Jonathan Trott is a former England Test cricketer who was ICC and ECB Cricketer of the Year in 2011. He is frequently called upon to offer his insight and expertise on cricketing on radio and TV, and is central to cricketing commentary across sporting channels. He currently plays for Warwickshire, having retired from all international cricket in 2015.

UNGUARDED

My Autobiography

Jonathan Trott

with George Dobell

sphere

SPHERE

First published in Great Britain in 2016 by Sphere
This paperback edition published in 2017 by Sphere

1 3 5 7 9 10 8 6 4 2

With thanks to George Dobell, the Senior Correspondent at ESPNcricinfo

A CIP catalogue record for this book
is available from the British Library.

ISBN 978-0-7515-6516-4

Typeset in Palatino by M Rules
Printed and bound in Great Britain by
Clays Ltd, St Ives plc

Papers used by Sphere are from well-managed forests
and other responsible sources.

Sphere
An imprint of
Little, Brown Book Group
Carmelite House
50 Victoria Embankment
London EC4Y 0DZ

An Hachette UK Company
www.hachette.co.uk

www.littlebrown.co.uk

CONTENTS

1

BARBADOS, MAY 2015
Part 1

How did I end up here again? How, thirty years after my first memory – hiding from the world after breaking a window at my dad's cricket club – did I find myself back in a toilet hoping nobody would discover me? I'd travelled a million miles and gone nowhere.

The sounds and smells were all the same. The gurgling of pipes, the odour of kit and sweat and damp.

But I was much changed. And as I looked at myself in the mirror, the sweat dripping off my nose, I thought of the toll that cricket had taken on me. I saw the crow's feet and sun damage. I saw the scar on my chin and the chips in my teeth. My hair had gone and, somewhere along the way, the fun had, too. Batting had become torture.

I had just been out for a duck in my final Test. I had hardly seen the ball that I gloved to mid-wicket. I knew it was over. Everyone knew it was over. I had felt great in the nets. I had felt great playing for Warwickshire the season before and for the Lions just weeks previously. But somehow, when I stepped over the boundary rope, I was gripped by anxiety and there was nothing I could do about it.

Alastair Cook made a century later that day. He told his wife he wished he could have shared it with me, and that we could have scored fifty each. He meant it, too. Despite needing the personal milestone for his own peace of mind – it had been almost two years since he had scored a Test century. He had supported me every step of the way and I was unable to pay him back in the way he deserved. I was pleased for him. But I knew my race was run.

Scoring runs had always made everything all right. If I scored runs as a kid, everyone in our family and household seemed happier. If I scored runs as a teenager, I'd be selected for the best teams and the best tours. If I scored runs as a professional, my team would win and everyone would be happy. People relied on me to score runs. They had come to expect it. Runs had always made everything all right, but the runs had gone.

I had always been a cricketer. I didn't have a teddy bear; I had a miniature cricket bat. We didn't go on family holidays; we went on tour. We didn't go as a family to the beach on Saturday; they came to watch me bat. My identity was as a batsman. My role was to score runs. I didn't have anything else to offer.

Generally, I had liked that. I had fallow periods, but generally I liked being the man people relied upon to score runs in difficult conditions and under pressure. I took pride in it. But somewhere along the way – perhaps ahead of the 2013 Ashes – the burden of that expectation became too much to bear. Every time anyone said, 'Oh, you always do well against Australia; you average ninety against them, don't you?' I felt the cold hand of panic grip my heart. Ninety! I couldn't live up to that! It meant I had to score 180 runs a Test just to stand still. Ahead of the final Test of that series – with the Ashes already won – I sat in my car ahead of the journey to The Oval in floods of tears. I just couldn't face going through it all again.

It never really got better. I knew I was going to retire after the Grenada Test. We had won and I had scored fifty in the first innings, but I knew. I couldn't do what I used to do. I couldn't get the feeling back. I couldn't get in the zone. I was holding the team up.

I wanted to give Adam Lyth some time ahead of the summer series against New Zealand and Australia. I phoned Andrew Strauss, Dr Steve Peters, the psychologist I had been working with, and Jim Troughton, my old mate from Warwickshire. 'See the job through,' Straussy and Steve had said. 'Do what's best for you,' Trouts said. I saw the job through. I felt I had to after leaving the Ashes tour in November 2013.

So, the job was through. And as I looked in the mirror, I thought back to all the teams I had represented over the years. All the tours. I thought of the U10 side I repre-sented as an eight-year-old, the U19 side I represented as a fifteen-year-old, of moving to England, of making my Test debut, of sitting in buses and driving through India and Sri Lanka and all those other amazing places I had been so fortunate to visit. I thought of the period when I was struggling for form in 2007 and looking over at the ground staff at Warwickshire and thinking, 'I wish I could get a job doing that,' and I thought of the instinctive reply I gave Andy Flower following my first Test innings, when he asked how I was. 'It's the most fun I've ever had,' I told him. And it had been.

And I thought of that little boy, aged three or four, who'd hidden away after breaking that window.

'See if you can hit this, little Trotty,' my dad's friend said as he underarmed a ball at me. I had been hanging around the boundary rope all day, hoping a ball from the match in which my dad was involved would trickle towards me and I could give it a smack. So I didn't need any second invitation when someone offered to bowl at me. I took a step towards the ball and smashed it back at him. He jerked his head out of the way and the ball crashed through a glass door behind him. Sensing I was in trouble, I dropped my bat – a chopped-off SS Jumbo that I used to take everywhere – and ran. The dark and quiet of the toilets seemed the quietest place.

And here I was again. Thirty years later. Hiding. Broken into more pieces than that glass.

This is my story.

2

CAPE TOWN, 1990s
Growing Pains

My mum had first taken me to a psychologist when I was sixteen. I had been pushing for selection in the South Africa U19 side but lost form horribly. My last five innings had produced four ducks and a 2 and I couldn't take it. One of my best friends – he still is; I've recently invested in his business – said something I didn't like and I head-butted him. Ridiculous behaviour that still fills me with shame. Anyway, my mum found out and took me to a psychologist.

It didn't take him long to work out that my mood was governed by my fortunes on the pitch.

'Why do you have to do so well at cricket?' he asked.

'I just do,' I answered.

'But why? It's not life and death, is it?' he kept asking, probing away like an accurate seamer who thinks he's found a weakness on off stump. Eventually I broke down.

How could he understand? Cricket had already become the way in which I defined myself. It was my identity and my purpose. It wasn't an ambition to play cricket; it was an instinct in the same way hunger is. It was everything. It was what I did and who I was. It differentiated me from the crowd and seemed to make my parents happy. I was so keen to make them proud. I could be a successful cricketer or an unsuccessful cricketer, but I was going to be a cricketer.

But perhaps each man really does kill the thing he loves. My reliance upon the game – the silly game where, if you were in form, you could nick a good ball early and be out, but if you were out of form you could miss it and go on and make a century – left me exposed. I needed it too badly.

I don't remember a time before I wanted to be a cricketer. Other little boys would answer 'Fighter pilot' or 'Astronaut' when they were asked at school what they wanted to be when they grew up. I said 'Cricketer.' Always. From the beginning. My first memories are of cricket. Other kids went to the cinema or the beach. I went to games or nets. It meant I progressed quickly as a cricketer, but in retrospect it probably left holes in other areas of my development.

Sport was important to my family. In the early eighties my parents had to decide whether to use their savings to buy a house in Cape Town near my school in Rondebosch or go to the LA Olympics. The smart decision was to buy the house, but the Olympics won hands down. They spent everything on taking the three of us to the US to watch the Games. I was there when Carl Lewis received his gold medal for the 100m.

I was effectively an only child. I had a stepbrother and stepsister through my mum, but they were older and, much of the time, it was just me with my parents. So I had their almost undivided attention and focus.

That is not to say I was cosseted. I was expected, from a young age, to walk the couple of miles home from school and it was instilled in me early on that, if you wanted something, you had to work for it. 'Never let anyone carry your kit bag for you,' my dad used to tell me, and it was that work ethic, that understanding that the game was tough and would give you nothing for free, that pervaded my attitude to the sport. Even today, as I watch young players pick up their sponsored cars and new kit, I fear that the game is setting them up for a fall. 'It's not meant to be that easy,' I think to myself. 'You're meant to work for it.'

My parents had both been fine athletes. My dad, who was born in England but moved to South Africa when he was two, was offered a trial with Leicester City; my mum played softball for South Africa and was offered a semi-pro role in Holland. Later they ran a sports shop together. Sport wasn't a release from real life for them; it was real life.

My dad was also a good cricketer. He ran a successful coaching clinic in Cape Town at the weekends and I always hung around, hoping one of the kids would be late or not show up, so I could have a net. I'd carry the matting, fetch balls and watch. At other times, I'd help them in the shop. I would help sand bats or stock shelves. I spent a lot of time with my parents. I loved it.

My favourite times in the year were when the new

equipment came into the shop. I used to love looking at the new hockey and cricket gear and I loved to watch my dad sell it. He was brilliant: again and again, I'd see people come in for a new thigh pad and leave with new pads, gloves and bat or hockey stick. He could have sold them their own teeth and left them feeling they'd got a great deal.

My dad made me work for any new gear. In return for a new pair of gloves, I'd have to put in several hours of work at the shop. I didn't mind – quite the opposite, really – and I think he was right to instil the work ethic in me in that way. I learned to love and appreciate my equipment in those days. When you sand and oil bats as much as I did, when you spending hours knocking them in – that was one of the services we offered – you appreciate how much work goes into making them. Years later, I was still the only guy in the England dressing room who could put a grip on a bat so that it was an absolute fit. Alastair Cook would always give me his bats to sort out and sometimes I'd sneak into Ravi Bopara's kit bags and redo all his grips. I can't stand to see them flapping at the top or exposing a bit of handle at the bottom. They have to be perfect.

I became very particular about my bats. I learned exactly what I liked – which is a pretty light bat with an oval handle and, instead of a large sweet spot – which is what most modern players like now – a bit more weight towards the top. I was never about power. Outfields are so fast that timing and placement are nearly always more important. I very rarely even tried to hit sixes.

I was first sponsored by bat manufacturers Gunn &

Moore when I was seventeen. Their rep had a good relationship with my dad and they gave me the most beautiful bat – a GM Autograph – in return for me agreeing to give them first refusal if I signed as a professional. It was the start of a long and happy relationship. I got to know the chief bat makers, the ladies who put the stickers on the bats and loads of other people who worked for the company. I loved visiting them and talking about the bats. I'd recommend any young player to build up that sort of relationship with your supplier. You have to ensure you have the best equipment, and generally the manufacturers will be delighted to help you find what best suits you if they understand how grateful you are and how much it means to you.

Many years later, I moved to New Balance. My brother works for them sourcing materials. I was the first cricketer they had signed and the deal was about four times what I was paid by Gunn & Moore. I was sad to move – not least because I had to buy myself out of my contract – but you have a limited amount of time to make some money as a professional player and the New Balance offer was very attractive. It took a little while to get the bats right but, before long, we found a way.

Anyway, one Saturday morning I went to watch my dad play for Techs-Mutual third team. The fourth team were playing on the pitch right next to his and someone didn't turn up. They had a hangover, if memory serves. So, with the choice of fielding a ten-man side or picking me, I was included for my first game in adult cricket. I was ten.

I came in to bat at number four just as my dad was going

in to bat on the pitch next door. Our innings ran parallel for the next hour or so, with me making fifty and him finishing not out 99. I have a particularly fond memory of looking over at him: we were both leaning on our bats at the non-striker's end in exactly the same way. He flashed me a big smile.

After I'd been batting for a while, a wicket fell and a new man joined me in the middle. He seemed about a thousand years old to me, so I took the opportunity to hand him some advice. 'The spinner is turning the ball away from the bat; just try and rotate the strike and don't try anything too aggressive,' I said. It turned out the new batsman was Denys Hobson, who undoubtedly would have played at Test level had his career not coincided with South Africa's exclusion from international cricket. He was only about forty. 'Your son is a confident bugger,' he told my dad after the game.

I was vaguely aware, even as a kid, that my mum was a bit different. We had a mums v. sons match at school and while all the other mums were pretty hopeless – they giggled when they were bowled by the first straight ball they received – my mum took it really seriously. I was used to being the best player in every game – I opened the batting and the bowling – but she smashed my bowling everywhere. I could hear the other kids laugh when she hit one ball over mid-wicket and into the swimming pool. It was embarrassing.

But I was also proud. How many other kids had mums who had played sport at international level? How many had mums who could give them advice and understood how much it hurt to fail and how important it was to succeed?

When we played against other schools, you'd hear other kids being told 'Well done' or 'Never mind' by their mums after the game. I'd get 'You're going to have to work on your running between the wickets,' or 'Your straight driving was much better today.' Sport wasn't about having fun or making friends; it was about winning. So when I had a cricket-themed birthday party as an eight-year-old, I wanted to bat through it. I treated it like a Test match. I couldn't care less that other kids just wanted to run around, eat cake and have a laugh. I wanted to get my head down and show everyone what a good batsman I was. I didn't want to make friends; I wanted to impress. I had the balance all wrong.

My mum was the one who would drive me to games or to training sessions. Thousands of miles; thousands of hours watching and waiting. How do you repay that? And she understood. If I was ever in trouble in school – and I remember one exam where I spent the time drawing the field placings I was going to set in the next game – or being treated unfairly at school, or if I reacted to a bad piece of umpiring on the hockey or cricket pitch, she would always have my back, she would always stick up for me – but if I was in the wrong she sure would let me know about it. Right from the beginning, she saw that cricket could be a career for me and right from the beginning, she guided me towards that goal. I suppose I became a mixture of both of my parents. I have my dad's patience and my mum's temper.

They were, in some ways, quite strict parents. They didn't much like me going out in the evening and there were times we would clash because of that. One weekend when I was about sixteen, my mum and I argued when she wouldn't let me out on Friday night. The following day, I failed in a game and when I arrived home she said, 'You never get runs when we've argued.' It was a phrase that stuck in mind and would come to have more significance many years later.

Knowing my parents were so invested in my career was a mixed blessing. In most ways, it was brilliant. It meant they took my cricket seriously, they encouraged me and they were always on my side. But there were times it felt like a burden, times when I felt painfully aware of how important my success was to them. As if the only way that the family would be happy was if I scored runs. I felt that if I failed the atmosphere would be tense and they would all be disappointed in me. The weight of that responsibility became counterproductive.

Let me be clear: my parents were wonderful. Hugely encouraging, utterly supportive and proud. They still are. There is no way I would have enjoyed the career – or the life – I have enjoyed without their support and their sacrifices. I owe them a great deal. But between us, we created something of a monster.

I don't think that's particularly unusual. There are lots of well-known examples of sports stars being groomed for success by driven parents: I'm thinking of Tiger Woods, the Williams sisters and Andre Agassi. The foundation of their success was the drive instilled by their parents: the pursuit of excellence; the identification of one skill that could, if fully developed, bring them vast success. But that demand to focus on one skill, on one aspect of life, can leave holes elsewhere. It can become a person's greatest strength and their greatest weakness. I can identify with that.

When I reflect on the dressing rooms I've shared, most successful cricketers have been the same. Do you know how difficult it is to reach the top in international sport? And how difficult it is to stay there? You have to want it so badly, to work for it so hard, that you make many sacrifices in other areas of your life. You need to have parents who expose you to the game young, then ferry you to matches and training sessions, support you, push you and sweep you up when you're broken. You have to be a bit of a mess to want it as badly as you need to if you're going to make it. There are some exceptions, but they are few and far between.

I recall hurling the ball back at a hopeless bowler who had just delivered one into the side netting. It was my school U10 trial and I was furious because he was wasting my chance to impress. 'Calm down,' the teacher or coach said to me. 'But this is my one chance,' I said. 'I've got to make it count.' I was eight.

I was playing above my age group level from that time. I was always pushing for the next level. Never satisfied with what I had. I remember crying when I only made the Western Province U13 B side when I was eleven. It seemed like a disaster.

So grand were my ambitions that, when Brian Lara became the first man to score 500 in a first-class match, I remember thinking, 'Ahh, damn it. I wanted to be the first guy to do that.' I would have been thirteen by then.

I was fortunate that my half-brother, Kenny Jackson, was just breaking into the Western Province side as I was developing. Kenny is seventeen years older than me – he's my mum's son from her first marriage – and a very naturally talented ball player. He was rated South Africa's number three table-tennis player and, once the country were readmitted into international competition, started to take his cricket more seriously. I would watch him net and go to the gym with him and learned a bit about what it took to be a professional player.

I also developed at every stage with Andrew Puttick. He was a good player who, for various reasons, has been unlucky to have only a brief international career, but he played a big role in my development – from every school team I played for, to the South Africa U15 and U19 sides, and Western Province. He understood about batting and how to win games and we spent many hours, for school and club, in the middle together. He opened, I came in number three and I made him run a lot of singles from the final ball of the over to make sure I kept the strike. We won a lot of games and I wouldn't have been nearly as good without him.

Another guy I came up against at that stage was Kevin Pietersen. He was a very aggressive batsman and an even more aggressive off-spinner in those days. I blocked the first ball I received from him and he barked down the pitch, 'C'mon, try and hit the ball, you useless ****.'

'Toss it up and I will,' I replied. The next ball he threw

up a little higher and I smashed it back over his head for six. He was unimpressed.

Kevin Pietersen:

I knew about Trotty a while before we met. He had a big reputation in age group cricket in South Africa. He had achieved quite a lot already and he was clearly on the way to big things.

By contrast, I was a late developer. And a bowler. I think he whacked me a few times in those days. I'm not sure if I ever got him out.

We first came across one another when I was playing for Natal and he was at Western Province. We clashed a bit. We were both tough and hot-headed young men. Typical South African kids, I guess. And there was a lot of rivalry between those two teams.

There was probably a bit of uncertainty on both sides when we met again in 2009. We had come across each other in county cricket a few times, but never really mixed. But he had just enjoyed that brilliant debut at The Oval and, after I hobbled over to congratulate him – I had my leg in a cast at the time – we hit it off immediately. I congratulated him and recall we spoke about a load of interviews he had been asked to do. All that stuff was new to him and I think he wanted a bit of guidance.

I saw that as my role with him and Craig Kieswetter over the next few years. As a guy brought up in South Africa, I had already experienced what it was like to be a bit of an outsider in that dressing room and felt I could help them through some of the challenges they would face. It wasn't that there was a split, exactly, but there were times you were made to feel like an outsider and I never thought that was healthy in a dressing room.

I think we understood each other. We had both developed through the same system. We both understood that, in South Africa, education was all well and good, but basically you went to school to play sport. That was what mattered. You played it tough, you took discipline seriously and you weren't sly to your teammates. We became close and it helped that there were two of us in that environment that understood and supported one another.

I was ten when I was given a job selling match programmes inside Newlands cricket ground in Cape Town. It was all pretty unofficial, so I was still meant to buy a ticket to get into the ground, but then for every programme I sold for two rand, I could keep one rand.

It didn't take me long to realise that, if I could get into the ground for free, I could make more money. So I devised a system where I would throw a handful of small stones at a bush on the other side of the fence. When the security guard looked to see what was going on, I would climb over the wall as quickly as I could. I wonder how many people have climbed over the wall of a ground on which they would later play Test cricket?

When England were there in 1995, I realised I could get away with selling the programmes for four rand. The only problem was, I had to make sure I got a fair distance away from my victims before they looked at the front cover and saw the real price. They were fun days and it helped me watch a lot of great cricket.

I had some great coaches as I was developing. Eddie Barlow was a hero of mine and instilled in me how important it was to toughen up, while Peter Kirsten helped me think in different ways. He was so talented that I think his advice was lost on some of the guys – they just couldn't do what he did so naturally – but I enjoyed his support and continued to progress through the system.

Progress wasn't seamless, though. When I was sixteen, a teammate from the club my dad and I played at, trying to be nice, said: 'You're going to get selected for the South Africa U19 side and make your dad so proud.' It was a lovely thing to say, really, but it set me thinking: they've given up so much for me; they're relying on me; I mustn't let them down; I must be selected for that U19 side. So when I lost form it felt worse.

By that stage, I already had a big reputation. All my personal pride was built upon my cricketing success. This first taste of failure – four ducks and a 2 just weeks before the provincial schools tournament – left me not only embarrassed, but without my identity. It was torture. I wondered at the time whether I ought to start thinking about giving up and spending my weekends on the beach like normal people.

My dad relieved much of the pressure. When I plucked up the courage to tell him how I was feeling, he immediately said 'Give it up if you want.' He told me there was no pressure and that it was a game to be enjoyed. If I didn't enjoy it then of course I could go and do other things.

The burden was lifted. Over the next few innings, I scored 66, 99, 38, 27 and 44 – all unbeaten – and, freed of worry and responsibility, just enjoyed the game without looking too far ahead. A month after I had thought about quitting the sport, I was selected for South Africa U19 for the first time.

It should have been a lesson to me. It should have taught me how quickly the game can change and how important it is not to look too far ahead or clutter your mind with too much thought. It should have taught me, too, that the parental pressure I felt was largely my own perception and that they simply wanted me to be happy. For a while it worked, too, but fifteen or so years later, I would have a similar conversation with my dad – this time by phone – as I told him I was leaving the Ashes tour. It was, I think, the worst moment of my life.

As my development continued, so the number of tours increased. At thirteen I went to Bloemfontein in the Western Province U15 squad, at fourteen I came to the UK (on my British passport) as part of the South Africa U15 side and by the time I was seventeen I was in the South Africa U19 team touring Pakistan. I always wanted to be involved, but homesickness was a recurring problem. It probably didn't help that I was younger than most of the others.

It followed a pattern. I would start a tour fine but, as it wore on, I would pine for home and a release from the pressure of constant performance and scrutiny. So when the South Africa U19 side toured Pakistan – where we didn't win a game – I started with a double hundred but, a month later, could hardly reach ten. If you look at the pattern of some of my England tours, notably to South Africa, they weren't so different.

Homesickness played a part in my decision to move to England. My dad's coaching career had taken off just as the shop business – squeezed by internet sales and an unhelpful exchange rate – had begun to decline, so when he was offered a job at St John's School in Leatherhead, England, my parents decided to move. It seemed like a pretty natural decision to follow them soon afterwards. It wasn't about money. It really never has been. And it wasn't about racial quotas in South African cricket, either. I played every game for Western Province the season I left. I just followed my family.

I have mixed feelings about the quota system in South Africa. I can see the need to readjust the balance of power in the country and I agree that it is important to develop non-white role models to inspire kids from every demographic to play this great game. And, if I'm honest, I think it's very rare that a really good white cricketer has been disadvantaged by the system. If they're not good enough to force their way into one of the places available, it seems unlikely that they would push for South Africa selection anyway. There are some compelling reasons for the quotas at development level.

But I also see some very modest cricketers playing at professional level. I've seen specialist batsmen sustain a career despite averaging in the 20s. I've seen a guy – Omphile Ramela – pushed into cricket despite wanting to be a doctor because he had obvious leadership qualities that were deemed an asset to the sport. I've seen the standard of domestic cricket and, as a consequence, the nation's international cricket, drop as guys are pushed into the first team before they are ready or when they are simply not up to it. That doesn't do the cause any favours. It won't inspire anyone.

Clearly the debate is more nuanced than that. I can see that sides might need to be obliged to dedicate first-team places to non-white players in order to force them to improve their development and talent identification processes. And I can see the failings in the system at present may be the short-term side effects of a sport seeking to correct decades of appallingly unfair policies.

But I'm not sure it's the best way to do it. Personally I'd have quotas at every level up to but not including first-class teams. And I'd work at ways of identifying the most naturally talented young cricketers from disadvantaged socio-economic groups – especially in the townships – at a much earlier stage and helping them attend the best schools so they benefit from the facilities, coaching and talent of their school colleagues in their formative years. If players aren't identified until they are sixteen or so, I fear it will usually be too late.

School had always been a stepping stone towards cricket for me. Early on, the teachers realised I was a sportsman and adjusted their expectations accordingly. While other kids would go home and do their homework, I would go home and knock in some bats. I was meant to take a book out of the library each week, so each week I would take a cricket book out and devour all the stories within it. I loved the books by former England captain Mike Brearley and still think I learned loads from them. I won a bursary to Stellenbosch University on the back of my cricket but, in my first-year sports psychology exam, I had to look at the board to see how the word 'psychology' was spelt. It wasn't really for me. Besides, by then I had started to play professionally.

I had some incredible fortune in those early days. When I played for Western Province against Griqualand West, for example, their team contained Michael Powell, who was captain of Warwickshire. I had a pretty good game – I scored a fifty in each innings and got him out – and won the man of the match award, so when he realised I had a UK passport, he suggested I think about coming to England and taking a chance in county cricket. Then, when Warwickshire played Boland in a pre-season warm-up game in March 2001, I made 69 not out – the highest score on either side – to help Boland to victory. It made sure they noticed me.

The first thing I did was get myself a deal as a club professional in Holland. I played for HBS in The Hague and, though the team didn't fare so well, I did OK and finished fifth in the competition's averages. The money wasn't great, but it was a fun experience and it meant I wasn't too far from England if and when a chance arose.

Looking back, it is amazing how often Warwickshire seemed to come up in my thoughts even in my early years. As a boy, I had kept an eye on the club's fortunes as it had been where South African heroes Allan Donald and, a few years on, Shaun Pollock played. Later, former England batsman Bob Woolmer, who I had known most of my life from the cricket scene around Cape Town, went to coach there and suggested I should think about pursuing my career in England.

It was still a big move, though. As I look back now, a wiser, more cautious man, I am in awe of the confident young guy who negotiated his release from his Western Province contract and crossed the world without so much as having a trial organised. It seems so fearless, so bold. Or, more likely, it was just stupid.

I had some help, though. Neil Carter, an old friend from Cape Town, had become a feature of the Warwickshire team and made sure my trial game – against Somerset in Dorridge – was on a flat surface with short boundaries. I made 245, a record for a debutant in the Second XI Championship, and put on 398 with Trevor Penney. Apparently I smashed my bat in anger when I was out. I don't remember it myself, but I do recall I was furious at missing out on a triple century.

I met Ian Bell for the first time on that trip, too. I had heard about him, of course, and we had played at the same U19 World Cup. He was only twenty-one but he had carried around this big reputation from his teenage years and there was a huge amount expected of him. I'd seen him bat in the 2002 Benson & Hedges Cup final, a game in which he played the match-winning innings, and knew he was something special.

I suppose I felt we had a bit in common. Both of us had been tipped for big things while still very young and both had struggled to deal with the pressure of that expectation at times. Anyway, I went out with a few of the Warwickshire youngsters the night before the trial game and Belly and I had a good chat about people we both knew and some of the places we had seen. When I mentioned I should get back to the Beechwood Hotel opposite Edgbaston where I was staying, he lent me £5 for a taxi. I'm pretty sure I've never paid him back.

It was the start of an enduring friendship. Belly was at the other end when I faced my first ball in Test cricket and he was there at the other end when we both scored centuries to ensure we drew the Nagpur Test and won the series in India in 2012. He was in the team for all but five of the 52 Tests I played and, at the time I write this, he is my county captain and doing an excellent job of it. He hasn't changed too much: he's still a bit shy and he still has a special place in his heart for Warwickshire. He may well be the best batsman the club has ever produced.

Belly and I both learned, over time, that it is one thing to possess the talent, it's quite another to convert it into match-defining performances. But by the time I came into the side in 2009, he had developed into a man to be relied upon. His performance in the 2013 Ashes series – when he was named man of the series and went a huge way to ensuring we won – was simply magnificent.

Playing alongside him helped me raise my own game. I aspired to be as good as him and admired how he reacted to adversity and setbacks. When he was dropped at the start of 2009, he worked harder than ever before and came back a better, more hungry player. The century he made in Durban at the end of the year was a fantastic moment for him and seemed to confirm his development into a top-class player. I've no right to be, but I'm proud of how much he has achieved in the game. Only KP and Alastair Cook have scored more Test centuries for England; only Cook and Alec Stewart have played more Tests for England; nobody has scored more ODI runs for England. He has had an incredible career and, returning to my hotel the night before that trial game, I couldn't help but wonder how strong this club was I was trying to break into if it had players as good as Belly vying for a first team place.

Still, I felt pretty confident. Bob Woolmer introduced me to Dennis Amiss, who was chief executive of Warwickshire at the time, with the words, 'Dennis: meet Trotty. He's going to play for England one day.'

There was no immediate offer of a contract, though. I went back to Holland, where I continued to play as a pro in club cricket, and it wasn't until the end of the season that I was woken one morning by a phone call from Kenny:

'Trott, get up. Your life has just changed.' Warwickshire had offered me a two-year contract.

3

BRISBANE, 2013

I felt I was being led out to face the firing squad by the time we reached Brisbane. I was a condemned man. Helpless, blindfolded and handcuffed. Mitchell Johnson was to be my executioner.

Certainly, that's how it felt as I approached the second innings of that first Ashes Test. There was no hiding the problem any more. I hadn't slept, I hadn't eaten and I hadn't been able to stop the throbbing in my head. The effort of constantly needing to justify my existence, of avoiding the slings and arrows thrown by commentators, by the crowd, by the opposition, by the millions on Twitter, it was starting to warp my thinking.

I admire Mitchell Johnson. He had been through some tough times, worked hard and deserved his success. He wasn't as quick as Shaun Tait – he was the quickest I ever faced – and he wasn't as good as Ryan Harris – who, alongside Dale Steyn, was the best I faced – but he was quick and skiddy and, by the end of 2013, he was bowling better than ever. He was fitter and stronger than he had been and his action, while still low, was just a little higher. It helped him produce steep bounce – bounce like nothing else I'd ever experienced – from a length that other people couldn't replicate.

I'd faced him many times over the years. He was in the attack when I made a century on Test debut. He was in the attack when I made centuries in Brisbane and Melbourne during the Ashes tour of 2010–11. He had been part of the quickest attack I'd ever faced – Johnson, Brett Lee and Tait – when I'd scored 137 on a quick pitch in a One-Day International in Sydney early in 2011. And he had been part of the Australia team that we beat relatively comfortably at the Champions Trophy in England in 2013. He was sharp, for sure, but I had always felt pretty confident against him.

The bowler I faced in Brisbane was a different man. He looked the same, but he was more confident, more assured, more controlled. In between the Champions Trophy and the ODI series at the end of the Ashes, Johnson had gone home, worked on his fitness and his action and come back bowling better than ever. His wrist was behind the ball, which gave him more pace and more control. And he was stronger than I had ever seen him. One day, I'd like to shake him by the hand and say 'Well bowled.' I don't bear him an ounce of resentment. Test cricket is meant to be hard and he was admirably ruthless.

The combination of his improvement and my decline left this an uneven contest.

How had I declined? I'd always moved a bit more than I should before the bowler delivered. At my best, though, I tended to go either forward or back fairly smoothly. Now, with the anxiety accentuating my movements, I was bobbing up and down and out towards off stump. There was nothing smooth about it. It was sharp and jerky. My head movement made it almost impossible to pick up the length of the ball and my body movements put me in no position to pick up the line. And, most of all, I had a headache. A head that throbbed and made it hard to think of anything else. I was a mess.

The first ball, bowled by Harris, is a bouncer. I jerk my head out of the way. I was expecting that. I'm expecting plenty of that.

The next one is fuller, on off stump. I play it out into the leg side. Later in the over, I whip one through mid-wicket for four. All the Australian fielders have their heads in their hands. I know, at my best, I hit the ball much straighter. But I'm falling over to the off side so much that I'm playing across my pad. It's gone for four and I'm still thinking negatively.

During the warm-up period, I had been in the indoor nets with Graham Gooch and Andy Flower in Sydney. So low was my self-esteem at the time, I was concentrating much harder on trying to impress them than I was trying to improve my technique. I had such enormous respect for them both that, at a time when my confidence in my game was ebbing away, I craved their approval.

It didn't come. Instead Andy walked down the nets and said, 'Trotty, what the hell's the matter?' Then he mimicked – not in a mocking way, more in confusion and to demonstrate to me how out of position I was – what I was doing in the crease: bobbing; weaving; lurching. It was grotesque. I knew I was screwed. I looked at him blankly for a moment and broke down.

At the end of the over Shane Watson, who I can't say I've ever warmed to, runs past. 'Get ready for Mitch, he's coming your way,' he snarls.

'Tell me something I don't know,' I mumble back at him.

I've played against Australia a lot. They are always like this when they're in the game: cocky; loud; in your face. It's when they're losing they go quiet and sulky. I've seen them quiet and sulky a lot.

But there's none of that today. They know they have something special in Johnson. And they know I'm struggling. They're circled like hyenas round a dying zebra.

Breaking down was beginning to be a habit. The first time it happened was during the Oval Test that summer. We had already secured the Ashes and I had batted twice in the match, scoring 99 runs in the two innings. I should have been pretty relaxed.

Instead, I found myself unable to face leaving the hotel car park. As soon as I changed into the kit we wore to travel to the ground, a sense of dread crept over me. I couldn't face the thought of going through it all again. All those people; all those cameras; all that expectation and scrutiny. I was so exhausted by the mental struggle that cricket had become, I simply couldn't take it any more.

Going into the Ashes averaging about ninety an innings, I had fallen further and further short of that mark as the series wore on. Everything I'd ever achieved was slipping away. I couldn't bear it.

So I sat in the car instead. I saw all my teammates leave. I saw the clock tick round to the time when I knew I was late. I saw the sun cruelly continue to shine despite my begging it, imploring it to disappear behind a rain cloud. Just briefly I considered driving my car into the Thames or into a tree. That way I could get out of the ordeal that loomed in front of me. I'd have an excuse. I could go back to bed.

Eventually my wife, Abi, appeared at the door of the hotel. She had been taking our daughter, Lily, for a walk. They saw me sitting in the car with a blank look on my face and came over to see what was the matter. Abi's words brought me back to reality and gave me the strength to drive to work. I knew something was wrong, though. I knew something had changed.

The next time I'd broken down was in Southampton ahead of the final ODI. I didn't want to leave my hotel room. As long as I was there, in my casual clothes, I felt OK. I knew that, as soon as I changed into the kit we have to travel in, it would all become real again. In the previous couple of games I'd been given a real working over by Johnson and, while I survived to finish 28 not out at Edgbaston, he had struck me on the helmet and exposed what was becoming a weakness.

Struggling with the short ball isn't the same as any other problem in cricket. If you are struggling on off stump, people talk about your technique. If you are struggling with the short ball, they talk about your courage. I felt I was being questioned as a man. I felt my dignity was being stripped away with every short ball I ducked or parried. It was degrading. It was agony.

I wasn't actually scared of the ball or the bouncer. I was scared of failing. I was scared being made to look bad and letting everyone down.

Kevin Pietersen:

There is something about struggling against the short ball that undermines you like nothing else. It erodes your confidence in yourself as a man. And, with cricket as it is, the bush telegraph soon goes around and tells every team out there that this guy has a problem. It's a cruel game in that way. Every weakness is exposed and exploited.

It destroyed Trotty. He had always taken such pride in being the guy who saw off the fast bowlers. He loved being our rock. You have to remember, he was a man who had grown up in the tough dressing rooms of South Africa. I think he defined himself by his ability to go out there when the ball was flying around and take control. But he just couldn't do it any more.

It blew his foundations away from under him. He doubted himself and even seemed to be disgusted with himself. You could see he was questioning what sort of a man he was. He was a proud, strong man and all of a sudden he was sitting in the corner of the dressing room crying. It was horrible to watch. Horrible.

It wasn't just the short ball, of course. But that's what people noticed and that's what people started to think and talk about. I think he felt embarrassed by that. He had other problems by then but it was the short ball that stuck out.

Ashley Giles:

I was a little bit surprised that sides hadn't really come at him hard with the short ball before. Maybe they had, up to a point. But not in the concerted way that Australia started to during the 2013 Ashes. It's usually the first thing that is tested in international cricket, but it was probably the case with Trotty that when he started he had the technique to cope with it. But by the time Australia arrived in 2013, he didn't. They came at him hard and it planted seeds of doubt in a mind that was already a bit more prone to uncertainty than most.

Abi:

His language changed sometime during the summer of 2013. He had always been angry if he was struggling for runs, but this was something else. He was distant; he was despairing. By the time we reached Old Trafford for the third Test, he talked of feeling 'humiliated' and 'degraded' and 'embarrassed'. He had lost sight of the fact that it didn't really matter. Not in the grand scheme of things. It was cricket, not a bereavement.

He wasn't even out of form. This was a few weeks after the Champions Trophy when he was one of the best batsmen. He kept making decent starts, but then getting out. It was all so unlike him. It started with the dismissal in the second innings at Trent Bridge, in the first Ashes Test. The umpire's Decision Review System didn't work properly and he was incorrectly given out. It just seemed that luck had turned against him. And it made him furious. Disproportionately furious and disgusted with himself.

KP was the first person from outside the family to notice there was a problem. He took me to one side at the Lowry Hotel, where we were staying, and said 'Tell your husband to chill out.

'Tell him I went two years without scoring a Test hundred,' he said. 'It will be OK, he just needs to stop beating himself up.'

Because of that, I went to the Durham Test to support him. I wouldn't normally have gone. But I couldn't reach him. Before then I had always known when to leave him to rant and rave, when to offer my support and when to give him a kick up the arse. But nothing seemed to make a difference any more. He was quite certain he couldn't do it any more. Eventually that thinking became self-fulfilling.

Midway through the ODI series, he took a turn for the worse. Until then, it was Ryan Harris he spoke about as being the most dangerous bowler. But then Mitchell Johnson appeared on the scene again and targeted him with the short ball. Jonathan's confidence was already in tatters, but now he felt his courage and masculinity were being questioned, too.

After only his second innings of that series, he said to me, 'They've got me and they know it.' It was the innings at Edgbaston. He actually finished unbeaten on 28 but he had been hit on the helmet – which he hated as he thought it represented something symbolic – and had a couple of DRS reviews that went his way. It was a scrappy innings but, instead of taking pride in battling through and surviving in a tough situation, he was defeated.

'It's the worst innings I've ever played,' he said. 'You don't understand. It's degrading. It's humiliating.'

When we first met, it didn't take me very long to work out that the gruff, tough South African that people first encounter when they meet Jonathan isn't the real him. He is a very soft guy under that harsh exterior.

It's pretty obvious to anyone who knows him well or spends any time with him. I've seen him in floods of tears at Warwickshire end-of-season receptions when teammates he liked have left the club. He cried when Trevor Penney left, when Neil Carter left, and when Jim Troughton left he was almost inconsolable. He'll be the one who will cry at movies or when we're watching TV. So – and I don't mean this to sound harsh – I sort of took it with a pinch of salt sometimes when he cried about cricket.

But this was different. He wasn't just upset or angry or frustrated. He was despairing.

He wanted so badly to make everyone happy. He

wanted the team to be happy with him because he was
contributing and his family to be proud of him because
he was winning games for England. It's silly, but I think he
feels people won't love him if he doesn't score runs.

Eventually I forced myself out of my hotel room. In the
hotel lobby I ran into Mark Nicholas. 'Christ, you're running late, aren't you?' he said.

'Oh, it's nothing,' I said and offered him a lift to the
ground. I'd always liked Mark and his conversation kept
my head occupied for a few minutes.

Outside the ground, I bumped into my mum. She had
tried to pick up the tickets I was meant to have left for her
but, because I was running so late, I hadn't done it yet. 'Are
you OK?' she asked. 'Yeah, fine,' I said. But I wanted to
avoid a conversation, really. I didn't want to tell her what
was going on.

I changed quickly and ran on to the pitch for warm-ups.
I was fielding in the slips and took a blinder, throwing
myself to my right, but I could feel the tears pushing their
way forward from behind my eyes. I could feel my breathing becoming shallow and my head starting to throb. I
could feel the control I had been struggling to maintain
for so long start to get away from me. I knew I couldn't do
it any more.

I sat on the grass under the pretence of stretching. But I
asked Mark Saxby, the team masseur, to stand in front of
me to effectively shield me from spectators and cameras.
The tears began to flow. I had to get off the pitch. I made
a run for the dressing room.

'Trotty, what's wrong?' Ashley Giles asked as he came to sit beside me. 'Do you want to play? It's up to you.'

I couldn't play and I couldn't explain. It was minutes before the toss. I had put Ash in a difficult position: he was a good mate, but he was also a coach that needed a win. We would have won the series had we done so. He couldn't afford a passenger in the side and, even though I was rated no. 5 batsman in the global ODI rankings at the time, I knew I was a passenger. 'I can't play,' I told him. He was very supportive. He always has been. England lost and I never played another ODI.

The England Cricket Board said I'd suffered a back spasm. That's fine; they were trying to protect me and I don't think any of us understood what was happening at the time. It's all very well saying 'Tell the truth', but sometimes we don't know exactly what the truth is. Within an hour of the match starting, I hopped in the car and drove home.

It was an embarrassing experience. I was one of only three guys in that side who had played in the Ashes and, as a senior player, I hated to appear so weak in front of younger teammates. I had been given the option to miss the entire ODI series, which in retrospect would have been sensible. But I had skipped the ODI series in India, so I felt duty bound to play this one. Few of the team would have known what happened at The Oval.

My mum phoned after the Southampton game. She thought I'd been unable to play because I was wracked with guilt over treating her brusquely at the team hotel. 'It's because of the way you spoke towards me, isn't it?' she said. I assured her it wasn't.

Ashley Giles:

KP came to me before the ODI in Southampton and warned me that Trotty was really bad. I knew he was struggling, but I didn't know the extent. I wish he had come to me earlier. I feel bad that he didn't feel he could, or that I appeared too busy for him to confide.

There wasn't any confusion: he couldn't play. It wasn't a dilemma. The guy was clearly in a bad place and his welfare was much more important than a cricket match. The game really wasn't in the forefront of my mind. We were lucky: for some reason – I think there was some rain around – the toss was delayed by about five minutes so we had time to change our team. I told Eoin Morgan right before we had to name the team. I think we said Trotty had a back strain or calf problem or something. It's not ideal to make something up but, in the circumstances, I can live with that.

Kevin Pietersen:

I haven't told anyone this before but, ahead of the Ashes tour, I had a chat with Andy Flower. I told him Trotty was really struggling and said that the one thing that he needed on tour was his wife, Abi. 'Forget ECB rules and regulations,' I told him. 'Let him have Abi on tour.'

Flower said he would think about it. But a week later he said there couldn't be any exceptions to the rule. It was typical ECB and typical Flower: bullshit regulations getting in the way of common sense.

Would it have made any difference? If I'm honest, I don't think it would have helped us win the Ashes and I don't think it would have helped him play the short ball better. They were better than us in that series and they bounced all of us out. We weren't going to win.

But might it have helped Trotty avoid breaking down to the extent it did? It might well have done. He is very, very close to Abi. He feels comfortable and supported when she is around and I think she's the only person – along with his kids – who allows him to switch off from cricket. She provides that level of unconditional support that means he doesn't have to worry about how he looks to the outside world. He can just relax and be Trotty. She's a great woman.

I always thought Trotty and I were very alike that way. Family is hugely important to us and, to perform at our best, we probably need them around. We need to feel comfortable. The ECB will tell you that, on an Ashes tour, they can join us by the time we play the third Test in Perth. But by then we've been on tour for seven or eight weeks and, if that dressing-room atmosphere isn't everything it might be, that is a hell of a long time to be away. On that tour in 2013, it was long enough for Trotty's condition to deteriorate to a point where, by the time we reached Brisbane, it could only end in a crash.

Anyway, after Trotty went home, we travelled to Alice Springs for the next tour match. Flower came up to me at one point and said that he should have listened to me, that I'd been right about Trotty all along, he should have let Abi come on the tour.

I just walked away. I was so annoyed with him.

I had been aware that my self-control was dwindling. After I was out in the fourth ODI in Cardiff, I had smashed the hell out of my helmet in the dressing room. It was the sort of thing I might have done a few times in my early career, but not since I had learned to control my emotions, and hardly at all since I had become an international cricketer. But I was so angry and confused by what was happening to me that, on the spur of the moment, my fury got the better of me. Again, it wasn't the behaviour of a senior player in the side.

As soon as the ODI series was over, I asked Ashley Giles to come to the nets with me. Every weekday, he would fire balls at my head for about ninety minutes. And every weekday, I would make a mistake every few deliveries that left me more anxious than before. What I really needed was a rest, but the only way I knew out of this slump was hard work, so I pushed myself on. And the more I pushed, the deeper I sank.

Johnson's first ball to me rears from just back of a length. Jesus, that was quick! It's smashed into my glove. My hand is in agony. I'm pretty sure it's broken. But I can't go off. There's no point even thinking about it. Let's get this done.

The next ball is short again. Of course it is. He's not going to let me off the hook here. Just as we didn't let him off the hook in 2013–14 when the Barmy Army were giving him loads and he was going through his own private hell. Good on him for coming back from that.

I feel myself walking down the pitch as he delivers. 'Where are you going?' I think. But I can't stop myself. I have to make myself move or I'll freeze. I pull and we score three. A couple of balls later, after another bouncer, I turn a fuller one into the leg side. There's an easy one or a quick two. I press for the second, making a statement about my lack of fear. Nobody is convinced. Not even me. Michael Carberry, who thought he was back on strike, can't believe his luck.

It wasn't always easy to ask for help. During a warm-up game in Hobart, the openers batted throughout the day and, after about eighty overs of sitting in pads waiting to go in, I asked Andy Flower if I could have a nightwatchman.

Andy winced in exasperation. He looked around the dressing room and asked if anyone wanted to bat. Finally he suggested Joe Root should pad up.

Joe, about a year into his international career, wasn't about to say no to Andy Flower. He put his pads on. But by asking Root, another batsman, to replace me, instead of the bowler that should have been nightwatchman, it seemed clear to me that he thought my request was weak. At a time I could have done with a bit of support, I felt crushed and humiliated.

I was aware, too, that just ahead of the tour, Andy had hosted a lunch to which the wives or girlfriends of players were invited. At it, he had told them to be unafraid to tell their partners – the players – to 'grow a pair' if they complained about anything on the trip. I knew Andy well. I liked, trusted and respected him. But I didn't always feel he was sympathetic to the pressures that we felt under.

I do not mean to be critical of Andy. I have a huge

amount of admiration for him. I consider him a friend. He did great things for English cricket and I wouldn't have been the player I was without his input. He probably didn't understand the extent of my troubles, either.

Besides, maybe he, like the rest of us, was damaged by everything we had gone through? Maybe he, like me, was losing himself in anxiety and anger and desperation. He was exhausted, in much the same way that Graeme Swann's elbow was exhausted and KP's knee was exhausted. But instead of showing on a scan, maybe it manifested itself in a short temper and an inflexible attitude? Andy had changed but I don't blame him. We had all changed by then.

He has always been hard. It was one of the qualities that saw his rise to number one in the Test batting rankings, that saw him seize a side that was going nowhere and take it to the top of the world rankings. But under pressure, every characteristic becomes magnified. And, over time, many positive characteristics can become flaws. So Andy's resilience appeared to gain a harshness and KP's relaxed demeanour might have suggested a certain apathy. They both cared and they both meant well. They just had different ways of showing it.

Clearly I wasn't on the whole of that 2013 tour. But I was there for a few weeks and, from what I saw, KP had been really good. He was making an effort to encourage the young players, he was helping the tail-enders in the nets and he was one of the few in whom I felt I could confide my worsening mental state. Certainly he was a far more positive presence than he had been in the early part of

2012 when the cracks were beginning to show. Maybe the problem was that those cracks were never entirely filled. And, in times of stress, the fault lines open up. Winning tends to make everything fine. But on that tour, England weren't winning.

This one from Peter Siddle feels as if it's on off stump. I play it soundly enough. I look back: I'm a foot outside off stump. I could have let that go. What the hell am I doing? Oh, my God, I really have no idea any more. I can't do this. I really can't do this.

Siddle is a fine bowler, but he feels like a medium-pacer by comparison to Johnson. That's why KP was to get out to him so often: he saw him as the weak link and tried to attack him. He tried to disrupt the Australian plans. He was trying to force them to bring back Johnson. To wear him out.

The first time I noticed something was wrong was in Chelmsford. England had a warm-up game against Essex ahead of the Ashes and, even while I was batting, I found myself thinking about the Champions Trophy.

We had lost in the final a few days previously. It was an overwhelming disappointment. Probably the biggest of my career. We had a great chance, the chance of a lifetime, to win the first global ODI trophy in England's history and we blew it. The final was played on my home ground of Edgbaston. I had been in top form – I finished as the second highest run-scorer in the competition and was named in the side of the tournament – with an average of 57 and a strike rate of 91. And we had nothing to show for it.

Maybe, if we had been given some time to reflect and get over the defeat, I would have been OK. But by the time we reported back ahead of the Essex game – the night before two days of training ahead of the match – we had been given just three complete days off. We hadn't debriefed or discussed it. I hadn't had time to come to terms with it. I hadn't moved on. There was no time. There was never any time.

You would hope that the ECB might have learned the lesson. You would hope they had looked at the premature retirements of the likes of Graeme Swann and Matt Prior and realised that the schedule was limiting the careers of their best assets. You would hope that they looked at the number of their players who were struggling psychologically by the end of 2013 and concluded that they were asking too much of them. But then you look at the England schedule for the winter of 2015–16 and you see that they have learned nothing. Even before we think about the ICC World T20, England's players had spent all but a week of five months abroad while touring the United Arab Emirates and South Africa. The short-term drive to maximise revenue is still compromising the long-term success of the side.

At the time, I put my lack of concentration down to the low-key nature of that warm-up game. When you have played a lot of international cricket, those games – and this one lost its first-class status halfway through as Andy felt Essex weren't testing us enough and wanted to draft some members of the England squad into their side – do lose their appeal and intensity. 'I'm turning into KP,' I laughed

My boyhood idol. Peter Kirsten was a friend of my parents and my coach when I was coming through the Western Province Academy. I spent hours watching him bat on TV and at Newlands. *(Shaun Botterill/Allsport UK/Getty Images)*

Bob Woolmer – here celebrating the Benson and Hedges Cup victory over Essex in 2002 – was a huge influence in getting me to Warwickshire. Long before I left South Africa, I knew I wanted to play for Warwickshire, where Bob, Allan Donald, Shaun Pollock and Brian Lara had played. It was always the only club for me. *(Philip Brown)*

My first-class debut for Warwickshire, May 2003. I opened the batting – it was the only way I could get in the side – and made 134 against a strong Sussex attack that included Mushtaq Ahmed, Jason Lewry and James Kirtley. *(Philip Brown)*

Leeds, 2003: my first time on the pitch for England. I was twelfth man for a Test against South Africa. It was a surreal experience. I knew all the South Africa players much better than the England players and, for a while, I found myself at third slip. I just couldn't understand why people kept telling me I looked like Vince Vaughn . . .

(Philip Brown)

This was during the 2004 season. I passed 50 eleven times, though I only made one century, and helped Warwickshire win the Championship.

(Mike Egerton/Empics Sport/Press Association Images)

Here I am with Car Lady. And hair. The day we were awarded the County Championship trophy at Northants in 2004.

My wedding day. Abi is the one in white. Jim Troughton and Neil Carter, great friends with whom I played for Warwickshire for many years, are behind me, with my old friend John McInroy beside them. Next to Abi is her great friend, Donna McManus.

Just before the Friends Provident semi-final in Southampton in June 2007. One of the things I remember most clearly about that game is how friendly KP was with me. Back then, we were never friendly to one another. But the day after the semi-final I was called up by England for the first time and realised that KP must have known. He was trying to make things more comfortable before we shared a dressing room. We became great friends. *(Philip Brown)*

Just before my England debut in 2007. I knew my hand was broken and was trying to work out how I was going to bat. It wasn't an ideal start. *(Philip Brown)*

I only played one Test with Andrew Flintoff – my first and his last – but I admired him greatly. He was one of the quickest bowlers I ever faced and he bowled so many tough overs for England despite his battle with injuries. *(Philip Brown)*

Andrew Strauss presented me with my first Test cap ahead of play at The Oval in August 2009.

(Gareth Copley/PA Archive/Press Association Images)

The moment I scored my first Test century. Look at the determination. I recall thumping my bat at the non-striker's end after completing my first run – the run to take me to my hundred – to make sure that even if I was run out going for a second, the umpire would know I hadn't been short of my ground. As it was, the ball went for four. *(William West/AFP/Getty Images)*

The stuff of which dreams are made. Celebrating my first Test hundred on debut in the match that decided the 2009 Ashes. *(Tim Clayton/Corbis via Getty Images)*

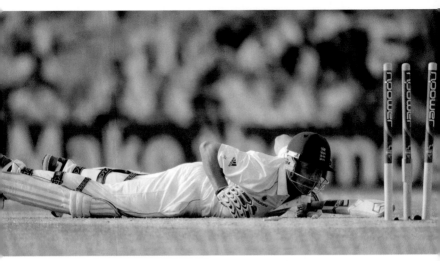

Here ends the first lesson about how precious your wicket is in Test cricket. My first Test innings ended when I clipped the ball into the leg side but Simon Katich at short leg somehow stopped it and threw down the stumps before I could regain my ground. It was an unbelievable piece of fielding and a sharp wake-up call about the standards at this level. *(Philip Brown)*

Walking back at The Oval after my first Test innings. The most fun I had ever had. *(Philip Brown)*

A great moment after winning the Ashes at The Oval in 2009.
That look of pain on my face is real, though. It's not so much
Graeme Swann strangling me, but someone had smacked me
on the back of the head with a champagne bottle. It was all so
surreal: a week earlier I had been playing county cricket in front
of a few hundred spectators. *(Tom Shaw/Getty Images)*

The first taste of Test
cricket. Celebrating
with Abi in the
dressing room at The
Oval after winning the
2009 Ashes.

The Oval, 2009. I
hardly knew those
guys at the time, but
I was to come to like
and respect them both
greatly. *(Gareth Copley/Pool/
Getty Images)*

to myself as I reflected on my growing antipathy to warm-up games. But it wasn't a momentary problem. It was my new reality. If I had to pick the moment it all went wrong, that would be it.

Kevin Pietersen:

I could tell he was struggling during the summer of 2013. The manner in which he was getting dismissed was one issue, but he was oddly disengaged off the pitch, too. Usually, I could always have a laugh with him but, as the summer wore on, he disappeared within himself. His eyes were elsewhere and you felt you could only keep his attention for a couple of seconds.

I'd say, 'Hey, Dutchman, when you going to sort your life out?' and usually he'd laugh and make a joke back at me. But that summer, he would look up as if I'd startled him and then go back to sitting alone with his thoughts. He was clearly a guy with a lot on his mind and it became hard to get through to him.

He had always been a pretty uptight, intense guy. That's not a criticism. It's just the way he was. He would put out his kit and his clothes in a very systematic, robotic way. But that summer he started to become really withdrawn and down on himself. He would punish himself when he was out. He was furious with himself and took hours to get back to normal. Far longer than had been the case in the past. It became quite a rapid decline.

Andy Flower:

I don't think many people who have played could claim they were unfamiliar with anxiety issues. It's odd but, as you get older, it seems to get harder to keep the doubts from growing. You are tested throughout your career and there are times you struggle and times you overcome. But the doubts seem to accumulate eventually.

I was relatively relaxed about Trott's state of mind ahead of the Ashes. Yes, we knew he had an issue, but we had known about it for some time by then and we knew he had managed it. I was confident he – and our medical team, who were very diligent – could manage it again.

He could have had the ODI series off at the end of the season, but I think he felt he would be letting me down if he did that. He would never want to do that; he would never want to take the easy option. I admired that about him and thought he was making the right choice.

But I started to become very worried about him in Sydney. He had scored a hundred in Perth and batted nicely. But he dismissed it as insignificant and seemed to be stuck in an oddly negative frame of mind.

Then we had a net in Sydney and it became obvious he was struggling. It just showed how far away from his optimal performance state he had become. He was practising badly; punishing himself and getting himself into a state rather than working on specific issues and improving.

Australia had started to target him with the short ball in the Old Trafford Test. It wasn't the first time he had been targeted that way – it's one of the first things that happens to any batsman in Test cricket – but he always looked as if he could handle it in the past.

It's never that comfortable when bowlers come at you that way. None of us much like it. But you have to give the impression you don't mind it and then they'll give up. Once you show you don't like it, you'll just get more and more of it.

This time, at Old Trafford, he showed a few signs of discomfort. And that was fatal. Once the sharks smell blood – and the Australian bowlers smelt blood that day – you are in real trouble.

Instead of concentrating on Essex fast bowlers Tymal Mills or Boyd Rankin running in – and they were plenty quick enough to focus the mind – my mind kept drifting back to the leg-side wide that I'd been stumped off in the Champions Trophy final and the sense that I had let the side down. I was the man in form. I was the man who should have seen them to victory.

It's funny, but when you're batting well, you hardly think at all. Quite early in my career, I remember giving an interview after I'd made a big hundred in a county game. I told the journalist that there wasn't much point talking to me at times like that because I hardly thought of a thing. I just batted. I watched the ball as closely as I could and reacted to it. It all seemed so natural and so easy.

I told him to come back when I was struggling. That's when he would learn more about what goes on in the head of a batsman. That's when he would learn about the worms of doubt that squirm their way through your mind and fill your head with thought and uncertainty.

It's the same with people sending you texts. After you score a hundred, your phone goes constantly. You receive texts from people you've never met and people you haven't seen for years. Sometimes you wonder how they hell they had your phone number. But when you're struggling … nothing. I didn't receive too many texts in Australia in 2013.

Johnson rarely bowls a spell of more than four overs. I should be thinking that. I should be counting down the balls left. I should be thinking that we're right on the stroke of lunch here. I just need to see us to the interval.

But I can't think clearly.

In the past, I've filled my mind with my rituals and routines. I stopped myself thinking too far ahead by marking my guard and adjusting my pads. I did whatever I had to do to prevent obtrusive thoughts. I go through the checklist to ensure there is no time between deliveries for any extra thought to creep in. I'm at my best when my mind is uncluttered. When I'm in the moment.

I started marking my guard in the way I do now – with a long drag of the foot straight down the pitch from leg stump – when I was seventeen. Neil McKenzie, who was four or five years older than me, did it that way and I admired Neil. At the time it was simply practical. Then, when I moved to England and started playing on slower wickets, I started standing outside my crease to help negate the seam or swing movement. The line grew a little longer.

I don't know when it became a mental crutch. It just built up. It remained largely a practical thing: I wanted to know exactly where I was. But I was also keen to give myself something to do to stop my mind from wandering and there was something satisfying about the trench growing ever deeper. It showed that I had, in every way, made my mark on the game. KP, who also took a leg-stump guard, used to say he didn't need to take guard because I had made it so clear when I batted in front of him.

I was aware the opposition would see it when they batted, too. I liked the idea that they would look down and be reminded of how long I had batted. It gave me confidence and satisfaction. They started to complain about it. During the South Africa series in 2012, Graeme Smith was moaning to the umpires before I faced my first ball. I liked that. It showed I was a danger; it showed I was bothering them. It gave me confidence.

Marking my guard was my medication. But now the drugs didn't work and I knew the opposition weren't going to be looking down in awe at the mark I had made on this game.

And Mitchell Johnson is starting his bloody run-up again . . .

The ball is short and down the leg side. It's exactly the ball he was looking to bowl; the ball to exploit my lack of balance. I'm so far over to the off side that I'm in no position to play the stroke I attempted. My attempted flick results only in a thin edge to leg. It's no leg-side strangle; it's clever, accurate bowling.

It's a lame end to the innings. And the worst thing is, I have to go through it all again in the next day or two.

That night I stayed in my hotel room. I ordered a bit of room service and phoned home. I wanted a distraction from the cricket. I couldn't sleep. I watched the clock. I saw it at 1 a.m., 2 a.m., 3 a.m., 4 a.m. My head throbbed and I started to panic at the thought that I had to get through a whole day's Test cricket without any sleep.

Finding myself so out of position to that delivery from Siddle had shocked me. I knew I was moving, but to find I'd misjudged the line by that much had brought it all home to me. It was, I think, the moment that my confidence deserted me entirely. It was the moment I went from thinking I couldn't do this any more to knowing it.

I had actually gone into the tour in better shape than I had been in before the 2010–11 Ashes. At the start of that series, I struggled with homesickness very badly for the first ten days or so. Abi and I had celebrated the birth of our first child a couple of weeks before we went away and I wanted to be with them. It wasn't until we reached the warm-up game in Adelaide that I felt able to get into the cricket.

Andrew Strauss:

I feared the Ashes of 2013–14 would be a real test for him. He wasn't in a good place mentally during the 2013 Ashes. He had nearly always been able to get back inside the bubble when it came to playing before then, but that series he struggled. And, at the end of it, he was rushed by Mitchell Johnson in the ODI series and wasn't able to control his emotions.

But you never know. I knew he had struggled in 2010–11 but then had a magnificent series. I hoped that he might have benefited from a break and that, if he had a bit of luck early on in the Ashes, his confidence might pick up and we might see the Trotty of old.

It wasn't to be. It wasn't just that he was out cheaply twice in that first Test, it was the manner of his dismissals. It became apparent that he was incapable of doing himself justice.

This time was odd. I was fitter and thinner than I ever had been. I even had the outline of a six-pack for the first time in my life. It's amazing what the benefits of being too anxious to eat will do for you. And I wasn't dreading the tour, either. I knew I wasn't in great form and I knew I wasn't as assured at the crease as I had been in the past. But I considered it a challenge and I hoped that, once the Tests started, my adrenalin would kick in and I'd be able to focus. Hope, though, is no substitute for temperament and technique.

I scored runs in the warm-up games. I made a century at the WACA against a pretty ordinary attack – it seemed to be part of the Australian plan on that tour to provide us with the weakest warm-up opposition they could get away with – and 83 and 38 not out at Sydney. But even after that, I told myself that the bowling was poor and the runs were meaningless. I noticed, too, that when we played Australia A in a televised game at Hobart, I was far more nervous. Those cameras, boring away at my technique, shining a light into my soul, were starting to weigh heavily on me.

For some reason, I had started to read reports about me in the media or on Twitter. If my aim was to gain reassurance, it backfired substantially. I understood that people had to give their honest views and that there were legitimate reasons to doubt my form, but some of the abuse on Twitter was vicious. Sure, there's support out there. But when you see people – sometimes people you know – questioning your courage, your honesty, your desire, the words linger. They gnaw away at you. Nibbling at your confidence. I never bothered to read the media when I was doing well. I didn't care. But now, at my weakest, I started looking. It was a stupid thing to do.

Graeme Swann is bowling and I'm standing at slip. There's no point me being out here. I can't concentrate. I can hardly see the ball. There's no spin – we haven't given our bowlers a chance – but it's just as well from my point of view. I'm not going to catch anything but sunburn here.

'I'm done, mate,' I say to Matt Prior. 'I know how you feel, Trotty,' he replies. 'It's a tough day.'

Poor Matt is struggling, too. He has been such a fine player for England. But now his legs are giving up on him and his form with the bat has deserted him. That's what happens when the confidence goes. He hardly has another good day in Test cricket. After all he's done and all he deserves. It's a cruel bloody game.

And Swanny. What a fantastic player he has been! His spin bowling has enabled us to play a four-man attack with a keeper at number seven. We have been able to rely on him in any situation: tight in the first innings, potentially a match-winner in the second. Jeez, he's bowled a lot of overs. Arguably nobody has played a greater role in the side over the last four or five years. But now his elbow is knackered by all those overs and the flight, dip and turn he once found have reduced and batsmen don't take long to notice. He's still a good bowler. But he's not the player he was. None of us are.

Australia are batting again having taken a first-innings lead of 159. Our poor bowlers, not given any chance to recover from their excellent efforts in the first innings, are given no more chance as David bloody Warner and Michael Clarke make hundreds. And with every boundary they smash – and there are many – they have a better chance to declare soon and put us in tonight. Oh, God, I'm going to have to bat again in a few hours.

I know I can't do this again. And I'm going to take it out on someone. 'Hey, Watson,' I shout at Shane Watson when he's out. 'Maybe you should spend less time worrying about my game and bit more worrying about your own? 'Cos you keep telling me how shit I am, but I notice you haven't scored any runs, either. You prick.' It's not highbrow stuff. But then he wouldn't understand it if it was. I wanted to go down swinging.

When did it start to feel like an ordeal? Some time during the Ashes of 2013, I think. There is so much hype before an Ashes series. Combined with the hype of hosting the Champions Trophy and then having another Ashes series only a few weeks after the first, there seemed no end to it. I seemed to be in a tailspin of anxiety and there was never the space to pull myself out of it.

In between the end of the ODI series against Australia and the Ashes tour I had three nights away in Vegas with my wife. I must have been horrible company. Too anxious to think about anything other than the ordeal ahead of me, I lay in bed immersed in my feelings of dread and barked at her whenever she suggested we do something more fun.

It can't be easy to be married to an international sportsperson. Your partner experiences all the moments of doubt and all the failures. They go through every setback with you, every time you are dropped, every time you are out of form. But when you have success, you celebrate it with your teammates. They get the champagne moments; your wife gets the hangover.

I run out to bat in the second innings. Everyone knows I'm in trouble here, but I'll be damned if I'm going to back down or back away. I'm going to take these bastards on.

A few months later, Alastair Cook tells me he could see the tears in my eyes when I joined him in the middle. But what could he do? He had problems of his own.

I clip my first ball through mid-wicket and we run three. David Warner is straight into me. Not much of what he says is memorable or makes much sense. Maybe he's a great guy if you get to know him. Suffice to say, I haven't got to know him. I momentarily wonder if he was brought up in captivity and if it might be kinder to release him back into the wild. Yeah, I should have played it straighter. But who cares? We're beyond thinking about the long game. It's a case of how many I can get in the short time I'm here.

That mentality had started during the previous Ashes series a few months before. At my best, I just batted. I didn't think of the time or the tempo. I didn't think of how many I had scored. I didn't look ahead and I didn't think back. I just batted. Sounds easy, doesn't it?

But I started to feel I was in a hurry. I was so desperate to reach 90 – the benchmark I had set per innings against Australia from previous encounters – that I found myself searching for scoring opportunities that weren't there. I found myself looking at the scoreboard and thinking, 'Only another sixty to get.' I found myself rushing.

It's telling that my target was 90 and not 100. Because this wasn't about success, this was about standing still. I had set myself such a benchmark that, at the start of every innings, my challenge appeared almost insurmountable. Instead of taking confidence from my previous achievements, I turned them into a burden. It's amazing how a weary mind will twist the good to make it bad.

Life had changed from the last Ashes series in 2010–11. At that time we were a young, hungry team. We were united by our ambition and few people expected much from us. We had nothing to lose.

It wasn't like that now. Australia were seen as such a shambles – they had sacked their coach, Mickey Arthur, at the start of the tour and David Warner was suspended after taking a swing at Joe Root in a bar – that we were expected to win. The reaction to our 3–0 success was underwhelming, to say the least. Where once it had been enough to have won the Ashes, now we were criticised for doing it with a lack of style. The level of expectation was so high. Unrealistically high.

Even the celebrations at the end of the series were muted. It felt like half-time. We knew we had to go to Australia in a few weeks and that the winner of that series would be holding on to the Ashes for a year or two.

As if the tours weren't long enough, we spent the final weekend before we flew to Australia on a team building camp in Stoke. It was the last thing most of us needed – certainly the few of us who'd played in the Test and ODI series – and it became a complete farce.

The course was run by former SAS members and was meant to put us in a situation where we had to spy on supposed terror suspects. In other circumstances, I guess it could have been fun. But it was poorly organised and wasn't what a team who had spent months, if not years, together required. They were a great bunch of guys, but the last thing any of us needed was more time with each other and less with our families.

We pretty much just sat around. There was loads of time waiting in a classroom and the food was fried and fatty. It just wasn't appropriate for international sportsmen.

The most bizarre episode of the weekend saw a group of players in a pub trying to keep an eye on these 'suspects'. What regulars in the pub must have thought when they saw KP and Alastair Cook trying to eavesdrop on some strangers' conversation, I don't know. But I do know I screwed things up because, when I was meant to be keeping an eye on the door in case our target made a run for it, I was talking to some autograph hunters. The suspect did a runner without me noticing. Nobody much minded. It seemed to sum up the farcical nature of the exercise and meant we could go to bed a bit sooner. I don't think that's the reason we lost the Ashes.

My abiding image of that weekend is of Boyd Rankin, knees around his ears, sitting in a Ford Fiesta, trying to look inconspicuous. When you are as tall as Boyd and his fellow quick bowlers Chris Tremlett and Steven Finn – and all three of them are about six foot eight – a future in covert surveillance probably isn't very likely. David Saker, our bowling coach, got fed up and simply went home.

I'm told that the trip before the Ashes series in 2010–11, when the guys went to Germany, was a bit better. But here's an odd fact: I missed it as our first child was due and Alastair Cook missed it so he could attend his brother's wedding. We were England's two highest scorers in the series.

Johnson is bowling at the other end. Of course he is. And he starts with a short ball. Of course he does. I pull. It's just like the first-innings dismissal, really, only this time I get a bit more bat on it and it scurries away to the fine leg boundary for four.

I attempt the same shot next ball but miss. The fielders go up for an appeal – well, some of them do – but I've missed that by a distance. I know, on one level, that I should be looking to get through this spell. I know I should be counting down the balls and looking to accumulate against the other bowlers. But it's such a good attack and there's no respite. Harris is a fantastic bowler and Siddle hardly bowls a bad ball. It seems impossible. I'm looking too far ahead again.

What's that chant in the crowd? Are they really chanting 'Kill, kill, kill'? Well, they may get their way. Would that make them happy? It would stop my pain. I guess it's better than the chant in 2010. That time they rhymed 'Trott' with 'vagina rot'.

Later in the over I pull again. This time the top edge falls between two fielders. It's just a matter of time. I shouldn't be pulling like this, but I'm so angry, so determined to show them that I can play, I want to smash every ball. I'm not thinking like a Test batsman should. I'm thinking like a fool.

I felt in good form going into the first Test of the Ashes series in England. I'd scored half-centuries in both Tests against New Zealand and felt good in the Champions Trophy. I made 48 in the first innings at Trent Bridge before attempting a drive at one well outside off stump and playing on. It was an unnecessary stroke and I felt I'd let the team down at a time I could have put Australia under severe pressure. Those who know me best suspected there was something wrong when I took a swing at the stumps with my bat in frustration. I'd never done that before. All those emotions I had kept in check for so long were starting to escape from my grasp.

Then, in the second innings, I was given out first ball after an umpiring error and the pressure started to grow. It was a decent ball from Mitchell Starc, full and swinging in a little, but I knew I'd got a pretty big inside edge so when Australia went up for the appeal I was confident. I was even more confident when Aleem Dar – who is a very good umpire – gave me not out. Even when Australia called for a review, I was confident.

But Marais Erasmus had other ideas. With Sky unable to provide him with Hot Spot information – they had been busy looking for a spot on Joe Root's bat after he had been given out caught behind the previous ball and hadn't had time to reset the software to use on the delivery to me – he presumed I hadn't hit the ball and overturned Dar's decision.

The Sky producer, Paul King, apologised to me afterwards. Fair enough. We all make mistakes. But now I had to score 200 in the next innings just to stand still. Now I was behind the game and I had to catch up. I felt the pressure increase.

In the following Test at Lord's, I had hit my first two balls from Shane Watson for four. The first was fair enough – it was down the leg side, I just had to tickle it to fine leg – but the second involved me reaching way outside off stump and driving through point. With my bat so far away from my body, it was a relatively high-risk shot for a man at the start of a Test innings. I felt in good form. But I wasn't in the right frame of mind. I was in a rush. I was desperate to reach 90. At one stage I hit Siddle for three fours in six balls.

But Test cricket is as much about the shots you don't play as those you do. It's as much about restraint as it is aggression. Just after reaching my fifty, I went for a pull even though I knew there was a man out there for the shot and spooned a simple catch to him. I'd given it away again.

It hit home at Durham in the third Test. I was batting against Nathan Lyon and I had 49. He bowled a pretty innocuous ball which, in ordinary circumstances, I would have worked into the leg side for a single. But, instead of watching the ball, my concentration wavered as soon as he delivered it. I recall thinking, 'There's my fifty; easy,' and, at that stage, stopped focusing on the here and now and allowed myself to drift into thinking about the future. I hardly played a shot at all; just nudged the ball to the fielder at short leg. I had lost sight of it. I had stopped watching.

It crossed my mind briefly that my eyesight might be failing. But I had a check-up and my vision remained excellent. It wasn't exactly that I couldn't see the ball any more so much as that I couldn't watch it any more. I couldn't remain in the moment.

My mind swept back to an interview I had read with Martin Crowe, New Zealand's finest ever batsman. 'I was the guy on 299 who swapped the mindset of "Watch the ball, watch the ball" to "Wow, the first New Zealander to score 300." I never even saw the ball that got me out on 299.' So this is what he meant.

Johnson runs in. It's short again. In normal circumstances, I could turn this off my hip for a single. But normal circumstances have left town. I want to hit it. I want to smash it. I want to prove I can play this stuff. I connect nicely with the pull, I completely nail it, and the ball flies off the bat. It's six at grounds in England or New Zealand. It's a shot that would have the crowd on their feet clapping. In Brisbane it sails into the hands of Nathan Lyon at deep square leg. It's a stupid shot. A sucker's shot. My last shot.

For a while I just sat with a cold towel over my head in the dressing room. I just wanted to get rid of that poison headache. Nobody spoke to me. We had all endured a pretty rubbish game. We all had our own doubts and demons to deal with. It was the end of day three and day four offered only defeat.

We took the team bus back to the Sofitel in Brisbane and, as the guys made their way to the lifts, I waited for the team doctor, Mark Wotherspoon. 'We need to talk,' I said. 'Can we go to the team room?' I asked Mark Saxby, who had become a good friend, to come, too.

'I need someone to start listening to me,' I pleaded, clinging on to his arms, the emotion already getting the better of me. 'I'm in real trouble here and I don't know what to do.'

'I'm listening, Trotty,' he said. 'I'm listening.'

So I told him everything. I told him about the headaches, I told him about not sleeping, I told him about the panic attacks and of not being able to concentrate when out in the middle. I told him about the involuntary movements I was making when batting and of my anxiety of being judged by the world. And, within five minutes, it was decided that I should go home.

'In other circumstances,' he told me, 'I'd sign you off for three weeks. If you were an accountant or a bus driver or nurse, I'd say "You need a break, take three weeks off and come and see me again." But this is an Ashes tour; things don't work like that.'

It seemed to be the only decision available to us. I was no use to anyone like this. I had given everything I had and fallen short. The game had beaten me.

'I have to ask you one thing,' he said. 'Trotty, have you been considering hurting yourself?'

The question shocked me. I hadn't. Not really. I had

considered crashing my car, but I always envisaged myself
being all right afterwards. Just a bloody lip or a black eye.
I didn't want to hurt myself. I didn't want to die. I just
wanted an excuse so that I could get out of going on the
pitch.

I went back to my room alone. My mind was racing
with the enormity of what I'd done. An Ashes tour was a
dream trip for an England cricketer, but here was I about
to abandon one on the eve of my fiftieth Test. But whatever
scenario I pictured, whatever solutions I tried to find, it
always came back to the same thing: I had to get out of
here. I had to go home.

I phoned Abi and a couple of friends. Eventually I
picked up the courage to phone my dad.

It was, without doubt, the most painful experience of my
life. I had to tell the man who had supported me through
thick and thin, the man who was about to fly to Adelaide
to watch my fiftieth Test, the man who had made me the
player I had become, that I was turning my back on it all.
I felt I was letting him down. That I was bringing shame
on my family. I felt sick. There was a pain in my chest.
I thought I might be having a heart attack. At least that
would be seen as a decent excuse.

'It's fine, son,' he said. 'It's fine.'

It wasn't fine, though. I pictured the kids he coached
laughing at him behind his back for having a quitter as a
son. I pictured him trying to explain to his friends, many
of them typically hard South African types, why I'd gone
home. He didn't say it, but I knew he'd be disappointed.
The man I most wanted to make proud, I'd shamed.

I didn't phone my mum. She was in Brisbane, but we weren't talking at the time as we had had a row before Lily's birthday party just prior to the tour and there was too much baggage. I couldn't deal with it right then. Her words from sixteen or so years earlier did dance around my head, though: 'You never get runs when we've argued.' She ended up flying to Adelaide anyway.

Kevin Pietersen:

I wasn't particularly shocked when he told me he was going home in Brisbane. I wanted to help. I offered to go to the nets and work with him, but I didn't really think it was about technique at that stage. Sure, he had some technical problems, but what was causing them? I didn't really think that trying things in the nets or working on his footwork was the answer at that stage. He was mentally gone by then.

We were worn down. The schedule of the England team does that to you. It's relentless. There's another tour, another series round the corner all the time. Your mind and body have no time to recover.

But it was the environment as much as the schedule. Flower didn't always know how to man-manage someone like Trotty. He didn't always know how to nurture that talent. And there were guys in the dressing room who were adding to the pressure.

He just needed to get away from all that stuff.

Trotty could still be batting for England now. If he had been better managed he could still be scoring hundreds for England now. So could I. Honestly, there is no reason Trotty and I couldn't be playing together for England now if the environment had been a bit better. If it was as it is now – with a limited-overs captain who encourages you to go out and whack the ball and coaches who don't worry about having meetings and just let you enjoy your cricket – we would be fine, I think.

The next morning I told KP I was going home. 'Don't do it,' he said. 'We'll go to the nets together; we'll work it out. I'll help. Don't do this, Trotty. There'll be no way back.'

KP had been the first to spot that something was wrong with me. During the Old Trafford Test, he called Abi to one side and asked her to keep an eye on me. He told both of us that I shouldn't be so hard on myself. He's a very caring guy if you get to know him.

I couldn't tell Cooky. He had problems of his own and he was still fighting to save a Test. I didn't want to bother him and I didn't want to let him down.

Alastair Cook:

One of the biggest regrets of my career is failing to intervene when I spotted the warning signs ahead of that Brisbane Test. I'll regret that horribly for the rest of my life.

There is one incident that sticks out. We were batting in the nets next to one another indoors in Sydney and he had the bowling machine set as fast as it would go and pitching short. He must have been hit twenty times and

he was being hit hard. Again and again, he was taking
terrible blows. It was horrible to watch. I remember
thinking 'What are you doing, Trotty?' It was clear he was
battling something much more than his technique; much
more than his ability to play the short ball.

I wish I'd had the confidence to stop things then. I wish
I'd stopped that net and insisted he tell me what was
going on. I like to think that now, as a more experienced
captain, I would insist he came out of the net. At the
time, and to my lasting regret, I didn't do anything.

Sure, I asked him if he was OK a few times. But he just
replied, 'Yeah, I'm fine,' and I never got inside to discover
what the problem was. I think he was trying to protect
me a bit, but there was no need. I wanted to be there for
him as he had been for me in the past.

In truth, there's not much you can say that helps
anyone in that situation. To some extent, we've all been
there and it is horrible. The only thing that makes you feel
better is scoring runs.

I think it was pretty difficult for him to ask for help.
His reputation in our changing room was as a tough guy;
the guy who would go out and spread calm when the ball
was nipping around and the fast bowlers were on top. He
had fought through so much and I don't think he wanted
to be a burden on any of us.

By the time he joined me in the middle in Brisbane,
it was clear that he had to go home. We hadn't had the
meeting to decide that by then, but it had become the
only option. I was a bit surprised to see him walk out:
as I'd been getting ready with Michael Carberry, I'd seen

him putting his pads on in obvious distress. I had a quick word with Andy Flower to say I didn't mind if he didn't bat at number three, but he needed to be in a better state if he was coming out to bat. He clearly wasn't and, by that stage, it was too late. He was completely broken and it was horrible to see.

The dressing room was an emotional place when he went home. He was – he always will be – a much-loved guy by that group of players. Andy was choked up when he announced it and, even as he did so, it felt like the end of an era. Trotty had been at the centre of everything that team had achieved and him going home was confirmation that it was over. I don't think anyone expected to see him in an England shirt again.

It didn't matter what anyone said at this stage, anyway. I was beyond persuasion. My mind was made up. I had to go. I was no use to anyone in this state. I was dragging the team down. They were better off without me.

I didn't know it at the time, but Andy Flower and Hugh Morris, the managing director of England cricket, both phoned Abi overnight. They offered to fly her and Lily out to Adelaide – where the second Test would take place – so I could have a break before the next Test. They said I could miss the game, play the game or go home. They offered to do anything they could. It was my decision to go home. Nobody else's.

The doc phoned her, too. He told her he thought I was suffering from a work-related stress condition and that, given time and support, there was no reason I shouldn't play for England again. None of us really believed him at the time, but it turned out that everything he said was spot on.

At the end of the match, Andy made an announcement in the dressing room. 'Trotty's going home,' he started. But he got choked up. Stuart Broad gave me a big hug and Cooky said he looked forward to presenting me with my fiftieth cap another time. 'That's never going to happen,' I thought to myself. A year or so later, when it did happen, he admitted he had never thought it would either. Most of the guys were pretty shocked. Every one of them was supportive. I really couldn't fault anyone for the way the situation was handled. Andy, Cooky, Hugh Morris, the Doc: every one of them was kind and thoughtful.

I boarded a flight at midnight. Kate Green, a development and welfare officer at the ECB, accompanied me. Within moments, I was asleep and I didn't wake until we reached Hong Kong. For the first time in weeks, I woke without a headache.

I checked my phone during our brief stopover in Hong Kong: nothing. Clearly news of my departure hadn't yet broken. The rest of the flight, which was in daylight all the way, I sat quietly and reflected on everything I was leaving behind and the new world I was flying to meet. I was confused and I felt guilty about leaving my teammates. But I also felt relief. Most of all, I knew that everything had changed.

When we landed at Heathrow, I checked my phone again. Before we disembarked, I saw there were seventy texts, mainly from old friends and teammates. All supportive and sympathetic. Well, there was one from a guy who, I guess, saw himself as a rival for my place, asking if he thought he had a chance of being called up in place of me. I won't mention the player; he has subsequently apologised. The first was from Paul Collingwood. It took me a long time to feel strong enough to respond to them all – I may never have done so – but I appreciated the gesture.

Abi:

I knew I wouldn't be going to Australia. It was never spoken about, I just knew I wouldn't be going. On previous trips, I would always pack a few things well in advance. Or I'd buy a few things I knew I'd need. But not on that tour. In retrospect, it was probably an unavoidable crash.

The team psychologist Mark Bawden called me after Jonathan had broken down during a net session. We had agreed ahead of the tour that we would check in with one another every so often to compare notes and see if there was anything to be concerned about. He asked if there had been anything that had worried me in particular.

There wasn't. Not really. He was obviously not in a great frame of mind, but we had been there before and he had found a way to come through it. We all hoped that would happen again, though I wasn't hugely optimistic. Looking back there were quite a few signs. He was so down on himself after scoring that century in Perth. 'It doesn't count,' he kept saying. 'The bowling was rubbish.'

I've no idea if it was or not, but you can't do much better than score a century, can you? And it's not as if everyone else did.

It's easy to say now that he shouldn't have gone on the tour, but it would have been a huge decision to make at the time. There's no blame attached to anyone. Everyone involved did their best with the best of intentions. They all wanted the best for Jonathan. It just didn't work out. Andy Flower's voice cracked with emotion when he phoned me. He was very kind. He asked how the family were and if there was anything he could do. Hugh Morris, too. And, in that very first conversation, we resolved to tell the truth to the media and try to explain things as best we could. A lot of bloody good that did us . . .

But you hear a lot of things about some of those guys and what people forget is that they are normal people. They're normal people doing their best in difficult situations that sometimes test them in ways where there are no right answers. All I can say is everyone involved in the England set-up at the time – Andy Flower, Mark Bawden, Mark Saxby, Hugh Morris and all the rest – was very kind to us.

I was escorted through the VIP area – a series of tunnels that take you far away from the main terminal and out of a back gate – to avoid the media. In different circumstances, it would have seemed fun; an insight into a glamorous world. At the time, it just made me feel like a fugitive: hiding and ashamed.

It didn't work, either. One tabloid newspaper had

already been to our house in Harborne. The next day, they waited in their car all day watching us and tried to grab me for a comment when I dropped Lily off at playschool. They would take pictures over the hedge, through the railings or from their car. A few times they phoned or came to the door asking for an interview.

I'd be lying if I said there were mixed emotions when I arrived home. I was simply flooded with relief. As I came through the door, my daughter, now three years old, said 'Daddy's home!' and ran to give me a hug. Then, after a pause, she added: 'Is he staying the night?'

It brought everything home to me: how long we are away; the sacrifices we make. The life of an international sportsman is glamorous and wonderful in many ways, but it comes at a cost.

Ashley Giles:

I didn't just fire the ball at his head in those sessions. There was an element of that, but there was a lot more technical work.

For a start, he had to re-focus his aims. When I first worked with him, one of the key aims had been to play international cricket. Well, he had done that now and he needed a fresh goal to try to reach. So we talked about that and agreed on a few things.

Trotty's technique had become a lot more open and, because of that, he was moving far more than he had in the past. He had always hovered on the front foot a bit, but so had Ricky Ponting and he did OK, didn't he?

So now we went back to basics. We went back to batting in the nets and getting him used to moving his feet in the way he had in the past. We started with full-length deliveries and built it up from there, so yes, there was an element of testing him against the short ball.

It was an uncomfortable experience. He already felt as if he was under a lot of pressure and I was testing him all the time. I remember being alone in the Warwickshire indoor school with him and a dad brought his lad in for a net. So it was just us and them in there. They wandered down the next net so they could watch him closer and it was awful. He was all over the place. He was upset, he was worried and he kept getting hit – hit really, really hard. It was an awkward situation. It was like watching the last thrashes of a drowning man.

There were moments we seemed to be making progress but we ran out of time. Maybe if we'd had a few more weeks we could have got him back to the level he had been in the past, but we didn't have the time and, if I'm honest, I feared for him ahead of that tour.

It was a perfect storm. He didn't have time to work on the technical problems and he didn't have time to take a break. So he did neither, really, and went to Australia with a weary body, a weary mind and a game out of synch.

To play at that level – against a really good fast bowling attack on quick pitches in the most hostile environment of all – you need your game to be at its best. If you've any doubts, any weakness, they will be exposed. And his game – his mentality – really wasn't anywhere near the level it had been or needed to be.

I've thought about it a lot: did we fail in our duty of care towards him? I think we probably did. If I had my time again, I think I might insist that he took six months off and missed the tour. I have a lot of regrets about that and a fair bit of guilt.

But can you imagine the controversy that would have caused? Can you imagine how angry he would have been to miss the Ashes? And how the media would have reacted and the questions they would have asked?

We did what we thought was best, but I'm not sure we got it right. We took a risk with him and we all wanted it to work out. Was it a risk worth taking? I don't know. But if we had taken him out of the side then, it would have been very difficult for him to get back in. There really was a lot of fondness for Trotty from the England management and I consider him a good friend. Maybe it was just an impossible situation and the crash was unavoidable? By that stage we were in the skid and it was pretty inevitable there was going to be an impact.

Andy Flower:

After Brisbane there was no choice but to send him home. He had been completely broken by that stage. He was unwell. There wasn't any chance of him contributing on the tour. I was surprised by how complete his breakdown was. We all felt for him. He was a popular member of the team and he had been there with us for a long time.

At the time he went home, I didn't think it was the end

of an era. I believed that we could fight back in Adelaide. In retrospect, though, his departure put the jitters up the side. He had been our rock for so long. To see him in that state was a shock to the guys, I think. And they were upset for him.

It was the end of an era, but it took a few weeks for me to see it that way. He was one of the last pieces of the jigsaw in that side and he was there for the whole journey. He came in as we were building, he was there when we made it to number one and, by the time we went, that team's life cycle was almost over.

4

CAPE TOWN, MARCH 2014

I thought I was better. I thought I understood what had happened and that a break had done me the world of good.

I was wrong.

I travelled to Cape Town in March to see an old friend. Paul Barker, a brilliant rugby player, had been my first captain when I broke into the school cricket team. He was a great guy and a man I always admired growing up.

But Paul had broken his leg playing rugby and, when the doctors attempted to set it, they found a cancerous cyst had grown near his knee that necessitated the leg's immediate amputation. We were all devastated for him and agreed to hold some fundraising events to help raise money for a prosthetic leg and a good quality wheelchair. I brought a bat and shirt signed by the England team to be auctioned.

While I was there, I decided to take part in the annual cricket match between the school and a team of old boys. I thought it might be the perfect type of light-natured game in which to return.

It should have been, too. I was surrounded by friends – I was batting at number six, my brother was at number seven and Gary Kirsten was number eight – the bowlers were schoolboys and there were no TV cameras or anything like that.

But as I sat in the changing rooms, ready to put on my whites, I was suddenly gripped by those familiar feelings of intense anxiety and impending doom. The trees around the ground took on the appearance of stands filled with people and, though the only noise was gentle chatter, I could suddenly hear the chants of a full house ringing in my ears. I was back in Brisbane once more: my heart was pounding; my head was throbbing; the claustrophobia was pressing on my chest and pawing at my throat. I was sweating and unable to think straight. I was that condemned man awaiting execution again.

I forced my way on to the pitch and, inevitably, was out almost immediately. These kids were bowling at something like 110 kilometres per hour but it might as well have been 210. I couldn't slow the game down as I had in the past; I couldn't stand still. I could barely see the ball. I couldn't bat.

As if that wasn't embarrassing enough, I went on to drop a catch in the field. I was running back from mid-off trying to keep my eye on a high chance but mistimed my dive and managed only to palm the ball over the boundary rope for four. To make matters worse, I had landed in a particularly dusty patch of the outfield and clambered back on to my feet with dirt in my teeth and my whites filthy, with the distinct impression that everyone watching was trying to stifle a laugh. 'They must think I'm such a waste of space,' I remember thinking. 'And they must think the England team is rubbish if I can get in it.'

But embarrassment was only a tiny part of the issue. As I sat in the changing rooms after the game, reluctant to see anyone, I understood for the first time the extent of the problem I was facing. Brisbane hadn't been a blip: it had been my new reality. I had a serious problem.

In retrospect it was probably naive to think that I would recover so quickly.

Abi:

A few days after he arrived home from Australia, I said 'Let's watch TV together.' He was feeling guilty about leaving the team and I wanted to take his mind off things. So I suggested we sit down and watch *Gogglebox*, the show where you see people's reactions while they are watching other TV shows. I thought it was the sort of throwaway TV that would make him laugh.

It was a mistake. A few minutes into it and we were watching people's reactions to the news of him coming home from the Ashes.

It wasn't that anybody said anything particularly bad. It was more the realisation of the enormity of the moment. This was Friday night at 9 p.m. It was

mainstream, pop-culture TV. It was clear that this
wasn't something that was ever going to blow over or be
forgotten.

   He didn't say anything. He just slipped out of the room
and went to bed.

The first month after arriving back from Australia was
tough. There were media outside the house and at my
daughter's school. At times, when they rang on the doorbell and I hid just out of sight, I felt like a prisoner in my
own home.

   I had never much enjoyed the attention that comes with
being an international sportsman. I liked earning the
respect of teammates and opposition, but I never sought
celebrity in its own right. I was happy to see the likes of
Kevin or Swanny gain the attention while I just went about
my job. The pictures and autographs that come with that
life were always something of a necessary evil to me.

   But at least on those occasions, the attention was positive.

   Now I felt hunted and judged every time I went out. I
could see people looking at me on the street and, through
the filter of my guilt, it felt as if they were questioning my
bravery, my sanity and my commitment to the team.

   I hated the sympathy, too. I can see that it was generally
well-intentioned – though I doubted it at the time – but I
had always considered myself strong and resilient. And
now people were approaching me on the street to stroke
my arm and speak in soft voices as if I were a sick kitten.
I loathed it.

   I didn't take it well, either.

'I know what you're going through,' a woman said when she stopped me shopping one day.

'I'm going through Waitrose,' I answered.

'How do you feel?' another woman said.

'I don't have a cold or anything,' I replied. 'I'm really well.'

'I've had what you had,' another guy said.

'Oh, really, you played cricket too, did you?' I answered.

They were all smart-aleck replies that did nothing to respect the kindness or concern in the approaches. Instead they spoke volumes for the fact that I was the one struggling to come to terms with what I was going through.

I tried to watch the second Test from Adelaide on TV. I felt awful about leaving the guys to do the job without me, but I wanted to see how they got on and we all had great memories of the Adelaide Test on the previous tour. But as soon as I saw them run out to take the field, with the huge banks of seats all around them, I felt that familiar tightness in my chest and my head start to swim. I turned it off and tried to sleep.

The next few days were tough. It was a relief to be home but, as I checked the scores from Australia, my guilt grew. My team – my friends – were struggling and I had abandoned them. While I knew I could have been no help to them in my present state, it crossed my mind that I should have remained with them to show our unity. I had been with them in good times, I should have been with them in bad. I felt terrible having left them to face the challenge. I still do.

My family struggled to understand what had happened.

I think they were shocked that I had thrown away something that we had all worked so hard to achieve, and a little embarrassed that I had been unable to cope with the stresses and strains of the lifestyle. For quite a while, they didn't want to believe it and hoped it was a momentary aberration.

My parents sent me a book – *All Blacks Don't Cry* – which was clearly an attempt to help. It's by former New Zealand winger John Kirwan and details his own struggles with depression and anxiety. But I think they were reeling from my decision and had a real battle coming to terms with it. That they tried to help in those circumstances is hugely appreciated.

A couple of days after I arrived home, I made a Skype call to my brother, Kenny. I wasn't looking for sympathy – which is just as well – but I did want to keep him informed and generally catch up with him. He is a great guy and was a very good sportsman himself, but he just could not empathise and seemed angry with me.

'You're not going to learn anything by sitting there and doing nothing,' he rebuked me. 'You've got to get out there and confront it.'

It was a conversation that really upset me. It was the moment I realised that many people, even those closest to me, would always struggle to understand why I'd come home; the moment I realised that many would also view me as weak and cowardly.

I hope that, over the months that have followed, Kenny has come to understand a bit more. He was an inspiration to me growing up and remains a big part of my life. But he is an 'old school'-type character whose inclination towards the stiff-upper-lip, macho culture of the typical South African dressing room rendered my experience some way out of his comfort zone. One of the key motivations for writing this book is an attempt to explain to him exactly what happened in the hope he will understand a little bit more.

Meanwhile journalists had started to ring on the front doorbell to request an interview, or waited for me to take Lily to school and then pounced. The ECB helped by taking out an injunction which gave us some breathing space. One journalist from a newspaper who had sent a photographer to my daughter's school was told he could have his accreditation removed if the paper didn't back off.

A couple of people who suggested that they knew 'the real' reason I had left the tour later apologised. Simon Hughes, for example, had tweeted: 'I don't think Jonathan Trott has a stress related illness. I think he has been freaked out by Mitchell Johnson. Reckon he'll be back in 2014.'

But then, in fairness, he wrote me a letter. 'I just want to express my sincere apologies for questioning your integrity and reasons for returning home,' he wrote. 'I got it wrong. I am a huge admirer of you and never intended to cause offence or distress. Despite having watched Test cricket closely for many years, I can only imagine how demanding the job must be. I sympathise with your situation and hope you feel able to play again soon. We miss you.

'I will try to be more enlightened with my public pro-nouncements in future.'

Fair enough. Which of us hasn't said something we regretted? But, fundamentally, I realised that, whatever else I achieved, I was going to be remembered not as the man who scored a century on Test debut, not as part of the Ashes-winning sides of 2009, 2010–11 or 2013, not as one of the few England players to win the ICC player of the year award, but as the guy who fled from the 2013–14 Ashes. This was never going to go away.

I thought I was suffering from burnout. I thought that, after several years of international cricket, I was frazzled from the constant scrutiny, the amount of time spent in hotels (nearly three hundred days a year) and everything else it had taken out of me. I thought I would be fine after a rest.

I wasn't the only one who thought like that, either. A week or two after I arrived home, the ECB arranged for me to see a psychologist.

He was a good guy. A genuine, well-meaning man who did his best to help. In some ways he did, too. I started to feel much more settled and confident and, by the time the new year came round, the prospect of playing cricket again was creeping back into my mind.

But he had never played cricket and wasn't especially familiar with the pressures of international sport. So he didn't quite understand the way in which the game can eat away inside your head. He didn't quite understand about the anxiety that can build up before you go into bat. He didn't quite get it.

Nor did I, though. As January progressed, I started to think of ways in which to plot my return to cricket. I didn't start netting as I wanted to ensure I had enjoyed a decent break from the game before getting back into old routines, but the thought of playing again became, if not attractive, then at least bearable.

It was about that time I decided to give a series of interviews. I had been inundated with interview requests – including some decent financial offers – but in the end decided to speak, at no charge, to journalists I trusted at Sky, the BBC, the *Evening Standard* and Cricinfo.

The aim was to get my story out there, on TV, on radio and in written form, to explain a bit of what had happened and hopefully put an end to all the questions and misinformation. There really was a lot of rubbish out there.

The *Telegraph* had just published a piece alleging I had been 'left out' of the Warwickshire squad for their preseason tour. Complete nonsense; we had decided a month earlier to give me a longer break from the game and I had never intended to go on that trip. But it resulted in Angus Fraser, the England selector, suggesting – quite innocently, but quite incorrectly – in another interview that my recovery was delayed. Angus subsequently apologised and admitted he hadn't been briefed on my progress.

Some of the rumours were far more bizarre. My Warwickshire mate, Jim Troughton, was talking to an England supporter one day who told him he knew 'for a fact' that the reason I'd had to rush home was because I'd just discovered that my wife, Abi, was having an affair with former England fast bowler Devon Malcolm. As the two of them have never met, that seemed fairly unlikely, but it just showed what happens when there is a news vacuum: people draw their own conclusions. I felt I needed to clear up some misconceptions.

There was no attempt to mislead or spin a line. Quite the opposite. I wanted to be absolutely honest and create enough space that I would then be allowed the opportunity to concentrate on my cricket. Sky's producers, having learned from mistakes made when conducting a similar interview with Marcus Trescothick, wanted the show to last a full hour to ensure the issue was explored fully and I had every opportunity to explain what had happened. It was probably a bit naive but I was feeling my way through uncharted territory. My intentions were good but, if I'm honest and if I had my time again, I might well take a different course of action.

The interviews were not entirely comfortable experiences. I'm not a man who is especially keen to betray his emotions but, while talking to Ian Ward, who I think does a great job, for the Sky interview, I was struggling not to break down. I was more than a little embarrassed about that being shown on TV but, at the same time, I was being honest and I felt people deserved a full explanation.

The initial reaction to the interviews was positive. I think people could see how much I regretted letting down my teammates and how much I had been struggling in the period leading up to my decision to leave the tour. I wasn't looking for sympathy, but I suppose I was looking for closure.

But then Michael Vaughan, writing in the *Telegraph*, said that he felt 'conned' when he heard my account: 'I feel a little bit conned we were told Jonathan Trott's problems in Australia were a stress-related illness he had suffered for years. We were allowed to believe he was struggling with a serious mental health issue ... but he was struggling for cricketing reasons and not mental, and there is a massive difference. There is a danger we are starting to use stress-related illness and depression too quickly as tags for players under pressure.'

He effectively suggested that I was looking for an excuse to dodge Mitchell Johnson.

Despite the fact that he never spoke to me, despite the fact he never took the time to find out what the problem was, despite the fact that he knew one-tenth of nothing about anything, he shared his views on exactly what my issues were with the *Telegraph* and the BBC at every opportunity. And all the while he used his Twitter feed to drip, drip, drip his views into the public consciousness.

It's funny. Michael Vaughan and I both batted at number three for England with reasonable success but it is almost the only thing we have in common. I have a bald head and chipped teeth; he has new hair and suddenly has brilliant white teeth. I think that's a pretty reasonable reflection of our differing characters.

Another *Telegraph* sports writer, supporting the Vaughan line of attack, wrote a few days later: 'Consider the anomaly, too, of the England and Wales Cricket Board issuing a statement to say that Jonathan Trott left the Ashes tour on account of a "stress-related illness", only for Trott to say in recent days that he was simply a victim of "burnout" ... he was just running on empty ... The explanation given at the time is not the explanation Trott is now advancing as he seeks to regain his England place.'

Isn't it? Are burnout and stress mutually exclusive? Could one not contribute to the other? Can they not co-exist? Are the definitions so black and white? If you drew a Venn diagram of the situation, would there be no overlap? Might the burnout issue have exacerbated the stress-related problem? Does a player have to be suffering from depression, not any other form of mental distress, to gain any understanding?

The *Telegraph* attacked me consistently over the next week or two. There was pretty much an article a day, all suggesting they had been misled by the original explanation for my return from Australia, that I had 'done a runner', hinting that my teammates had turned against me and that no captain would trust me. Just look at the headlines in the picture section. Well, here we are, more than two years later, and both my Test captains have contributed to this book and no player from that tour has said anything of the sort.

It was also a pretty surprising reaction from a paper that had promised me positive coverage (they were, their sports editor claimed in an email to my agent, 'a paper that treats situations like these sensitively ... and would make you think of us to speak to when the time is right') if I gave them my first interview. What was their agenda? Maybe it was a case of punishing me for my decision not to go with them?

I was disappointed with Piers Morgan, too. He said something along the lines of me quitting the Ashes tour because I couldn't handle the pace of Mitchell Johnson and spoke with remarkable authority when he stated I 'wasn't depressed or mentally ill'.

'He quit and went home,' he said. 'That may sound harsh but we aren't talking about somebody suffering from acute mental illness because if we were he wouldn't be back in the reckoning. It was lightning fast bowling on quick pitches and he couldn't handle it.'

I don't know Piers at all – and vice versa, of course – and I'm reasonably sure we've never met. We have a mutual friend in KP, who speaks very highly of him, but to come to those conclusions at a distance and then have the certainty to broadcast them as if they were informed and factual seemed fairly extraordinary to me. And, at the time, it really wasn't very helpful.

To be fair to Piers, I don't think he was meaning to be critical of me. He was more interested in making a point about the treatment of KP and used the ECB's willingness to welcome me back in contrast to their attitude towards him. I can see that.

But by doing so, he perpetuated the lazy generalisation that these stress-related conditions are just a sign of weakness. While probably not realising it, he made it harder for other people – be they in entertainment, or law, or nursing or teaching – to open up and discuss their problems as they risked being dismissed in the same way I was.

The thing is, Piers has a fantastic platform from which he can shape views. He can use his five million Twitter followers and his column in a national newspaper to educate and inform. He can use it to do good. I've actually admired the way he used that platform to push for gun control in the US.

Instead he used it to demean and diminish.

I wish he had picked up the phone. I wish he had asked me what I was going through. I still do. I don't want to berate him or argue; I want to give him my side of what happened and maybe, as a consequence, leave him a bit better informed – and a bit less critical – next time something similar happens.

If we really are serious, as a society, about helping people with mental health issues, our media has try to judge a little less and understand a little more.

But it was the Vaughan criticism that was the most damaging.

I began to question if he had an agenda as well. Vaughan, as a highly respected and successful former captain of England, had several strong platforms on which to share his views. As well as being a high-profile summariser for the BBC and analyst for the *Telegraph*, he was also Business Development Manager for ISM, a sports management agency. His own website – and his profile on the ISM website – stated: 'He also fulfils an important role guiding the young players on ISM's book as the Business Development Manager.' ISM had an interest in several players on the verge of the England sides. So if I was out of the way – and Vaughan's scorn for my condition made it quite clear that he thought I should be banished for ever – might there be more room in the side for the likes of Joe Root, Jonny Bairstow (who was with them at the time but isn't now), Scott Borthwick and Ben Stokes?

Only Michael Vaughan can tell you for sure whether he was influenced by that relationship. But it shocked me that the BBC and the *Telegraph* continued to use him as an analyst despite the possibility of the perception of a conflict of interest. Surely there should have been a disclaimer at the end of every article he wrote or every show on which he appeared letting the public know the context of his views?

Anyway, at the time, it felt as if Vaughan were trying to crush me when I was down.

My poor relationship with him had its roots in an incident from years earlier – it wasn't the first time that he'd had a go at me. In his book – published towards the end of 2009 – he said he saw me celebrating with South Africa's players after they defeated England at Edgbaston in 2008. The inference was that I was not truly committed to England. Indeed, he claimed it was 'a sad day for English cricket'.

It was rubbish. I had rushed back from Leicestershire, where I had been playing with Warwickshire, to witness what I thought would be a tight finish in the Test between England and South Africa. There were several guys playing in that match who I considered good friends – guys on both sides – but there was no question that I wanted England to win.

The place was packed when we arrived, so we stood in between the dressing rooms. This was before the redevelopment of the ground, so there was a gap between two stands – the pavilion, where the England dressing room was situated, and the Ryder Stand where the South Africa team were based – from where we watched.

Anyway, I was standing between the dressing rooms with my Warwickshire colleagues Neil Carter and Allan Donald. AD, of course, was supporting South Africa. When South Africa won, he exchanged high-fives with a few of their guys, but I hung back a bit and had no part in it. After the presentations and after the crowd left, I said hi to a few guys – Dale Steyn, who had played for Warwickshire, and Paul Harris, who I had known growing up – and caught up with my Warwickshire colleagues who had been involved in the match, Ian Bell and Tim Ambrose.

I then went closer to the England dressing room, where I caught up with the highly popular dressing-room attendant, Roy French, when Vaughan pushed past me on the way to the press conference at which he was to resign the captaincy. By the time he returned I had gone in to the Warwickshire offices – my wife had worked there as press officer when I first joined the club and I had several friends there – and I suppose he heard the sounds of celebration from the South African dressing room and presumed that I was part of it.

Later, I was sitting on my couch at home when I received a text from Ashley Giles. 'Are you out with the South Africa team?' he asked. You can guess who might have told him I was. 'Of course not,' I replied.

I had never felt conflicted about my allegiance to England. I feel incredibly grateful for my upbringing in South Africa, where sport is taken more seriously than it is in England and I had the chance to play pretty much all year round, but my life had long since been about England. I had married an English girl, we were raising our family in Birmingham and I was utterly committed to Warwickshire, where I had played among friends for many years. I had always supported England – and Spurs – in football.

Just before the Champions Trophy, I had given an interview where I had said something about preferring Birmingham to Cape Town. It provoked a fairly predictable response in South Africa, but I meant it. That was not to decry Cape Town, which is clearly a special city with beautiful features and a place that will always hold special memories for me, but more a sense that I had found a home at Warwickshire and in Birmingham and it was where I saw us living the rest of our lives. I had never been a Kolpak registration, either. I had a UK passport from the start. Like a million others who moved here, I felt completely British.

Why did Vaughan write what he did? I don't know. Maybe it was a misunderstanding? Maybe he felt threatened by my emergence and felt the need to discredit me? Maybe he was just trying to increase sales of his book? I was pretty topical at the time – I had just made a century on Test debut at The Oval to help us clinch the Ashes – and his story was included in the serialisation that appeared in a newspaper. Whatever the reason, it wasn't correct and there are many witnesses who can confirm that. Among them was Graeme Smith, who dismissed the story as 'absolute rubbish' in a radio interview.

I read a good piece a few weeks ago. It was written by a guy called Matthew Stadlen, a journalist who had suffered similar anxiety problems. It was part of a series encouraging men to talk about their mental health issues.

And do you know where I read it? The *Telegraph*.

Maybe they've changed as a newspaper. But in my experience, when I tried to talk about my mental health issues, they responded with judgement and criticism. At my most vulnerable, they put the boot in. When I was on the edge, they almost pushed me over. They supported KP, now a columnist at the paper, when he said he was being bullied in the England dressing room, but how do they reflect on their treatment of me? It felt like bullying from where I was sitting.

I write this now with trepidation. An individual can never win when they take on the media – or even a section of the media; most journalists treated the situation fairly – and I guess there may be a backlash from the *Telegraph* when this is published. But I reiterate: if we want to see greater understanding of mental health issues we all – the media included – have to act with a little restraint in such situations. I'm tired of being frightened about what people think or say. I'm not going to be intimidated by what the *Telegraph* might say any more.

Abi:

The lowest point in the whole episode came after the Sky documentary was aired.

The immediate aftermath – during the broadcast and right afterwards – was overwhelmingly positive.

But then Michael Vaughan's pieces changed the narrative. We were accused of conning people or trying to

cover up the truth. He was accused of doing a runner and
being selfish.

The vitriol that was poured upon Jonathan in the
days and weeks that followed was incredible. And this
was a man who was struggling to cope anyway. He was
devastated. He really was. And I was worried about him.
It's the lowest I've ever seen him. I didn't think he could
take any more hurt.

I think it was the accusation of selfishness that
hurt most. It was the concern that he was letting his
teammates down that drove him to the brink in the
first place. He was so determined to contribute to their
success that he couldn't bear the idea that he was failing
them.

We had no voice, no ability to reply. It felt as if we were
trapped in a cage while people threw stones at us. The
media were the hunters and we were their prey. It was
the most horrible experience of our lives. I felt we were
treated like criminals.

And what had we done? He had been ill and we had
tried to explain it. I couldn't see what caused the depth of
abuse.

Stuart Broad, who Jonathan really likes, texted during
that period. 'The whole team are with you,' he said.
'Don't believe anyone who says otherwise.' Jonathan
won't tell anyone that sort of thing, because he sees it
as private. But it was a real boost to him in some of his
darkest days.

That was one of the benefits of the experience. You
learn who your friends are in such moments and we

With two great characters: Graeme Swann and Liam Plunkett. I'm a big fan of both of them. *(Philip Brown)*

Getting to know Andy Flower in South Africa, December 2009. Andy is an excellent batting coach and a huge part of the reason that team made it to number one in the world in all formats. And, if he was a bit severe in his last few months as coach, I feel it's only because he was as exhausted as the rest of us. *(Philip Brown)*

A poor man's Jacques Kallis appeals
for LBW against . . . Jacques Kallis.
Was it out? Was it hell. He was far
too good. *(Philip Brown)*

Maybe the best ball I ever received.
And the one that ended my Cape
Town dreams. Dale Steyn managed
to gain some sharp reverse swing
and the ball nipped between my bat
and pad. I made 42. *(Philip Brown)*

Pulling a boundary at Lord's on the way to a double-century against Bangladesh. The innings clinched my place in the team. I was batting with KP when I reached my hundred and remember saying, 'That must be the best feeling in the world.' *(Philip Brown)*

My first Test wicket. Bangladesh's Jahurul Islam had squeezed one into his pad and it ballooned back to me. I only took four more Test wickets. *(Philip Brown)*

Making my first ODI century against Bangladesh at Edgbaston in July 2010. I had scored 94 against the same side a couple of days previously in a game we lost and knew I had to prove myself if I was going to earn a regular place in the side. I made half-centuries – at least – in five successive innings and six in seven games and secured that number-three position for the next few years. *(Philip Brown)*

The first use of the Umpire Decision Review System in England. I had been adjudged leg before against Danish Kaneria at Trent Bridge in 2010 but knew I had hit the ball. Reviews proved it and the decision was overturned. I had less luck with DRS at the same ground in 2013.

(Philip Brown)

Another proud moment: at the end of the second day of the Lord's Test against Pakistan in 2010. Stuart Broad and I had both made centuries and were well on the way to establishing a world-record eighth-wicket stand of 322. Probably my best Test innings technically. The bowling and the conditions were hugely challenging – we had been 102 for seven – and Stuart showed what a naturally talented batsman he was. I'll always remember walking through the Long Room: the members had formed a tunnel and were cheering and patting us on the back. *(Philip Brown)*

Reaching my century at Lord's. I was on 99 and pushed the ball for a sharp single. Umar Akmal, who had been giving me abuse all innings, picked up and threw but the ball hit my bat and sped away to the boundary, so I reached my century with a five. I vaguely recall congratulating him on his throw. *(Philip Brown)*

The Ashes squad ahead of the 2010–11 tour. We had the confidence, experience and spirit to beat Australia and we knew it. *(Julian Finney/Getty Images)*

My proudest moment. I have a huge canvas of this picture on the wall at home. It brings back a lot of happy memories. I had worked so hard on my fielding. It was the fourth ball of the Adelaide Test in 2010. Shane Watson had squeezed the ball out into the leg side and I had run to it, picked it up and thrown with pretty much one stump to aim at and run out Simon Katich. We got Ricky Ponting next ball and had them two down before they had scored a run. *(Tom Shaw/Getty Images)*

The moment I was hit on the leg in Melbourne in 2010. Andy Flower responded to my requests for treatment by suggesting I toughen up. I'll teach him who's tough, I thought. He knew just which buttons to press to get the best out of me. *(Philip Brown)*

Pulling Mitchell Johnson for four during the Ashes of 2010–11. I made two Ashes tours to Australia. I hope people don't just remember the second one. *(Philip Brown)*

It may seem strange, but the moment I reached my century in Melbourne was the moment I felt I had arrived in Test cricket. It was my fourth Test century and I recall looking up, feeling the sun on my face and thinking of my grandfather who had passed away not long before. We knew the Ashes were ours and I knew I had contributed. *(Tom Shaw/Getty Images)*

turned out to have quite a few. I'm so grateful for the support of Ruth Strauss, Ann Bevan, and both Jim and Naomi Troughton. At other times Chantal Bell and Karen Moores were brilliant. Knowing Mark Saxby was on tour with Jonathan was always a relief. I knew he would look out for him. I knew he would call if he thought things were deteriorating to a state where we needed to act. All the people I thought I could rely upon, old friends who had been there for years, were brilliant. They all understood how painful it was to see your husband dragged through the mud. With their help, I found the strength to pull through and continue to support Jonathan.

I wrote a letter to Michael Vaughan at the time but never posted it. I might give it to him one day. It's not horrid or abusive or anything like that. It just makes it plain how much damage he caused. I wanted him to know the extent of the hurt his ill-considered words caused to our family. I wanted him to reflect on how he would feel if the shoe was on the other foot: how he would feel if it was his family who was being slaughtered in the media. And I wanted to ask him how he had suddenly become such an expert on mental health matters.

He doesn't know Jonathan at all. They've hardly ever spoken. Yet he spoke as if he knew what was going on.

The irony of the whole thing was, we had set out only to tell the truth. We did the Sky show to answer the questions that were out there. We did it to clear up the misconceptions that were building up. We couldn't have

been more open and honest. I always thought honesty
is the best policy. But it wasn't, really. It just caused us
more pain. He deserved a lot better. He tried to open up
about something very personal and very painful to him
and he was accused of making it up. He had exposed his
vulnerability just to see people use it as an opportunity to
hurt him.

This whole episode has been a learning experience for me
as much as anyone. Part of the criticism of my Sky interview centred upon a couple of phrases I used. Specifically,
I said I wasn't 'crazy' or 'a nutcase'. If I had my time again,
I would pick my words more carefully. And I'm happy
to take this opportunity to apologise for any offence that
was caused; it was clumsy terminology and in no way
reflects my opinion of anyone who suffers from mental
health issues.

It bewildered me a bit that people suggested I was talking about depression when I used those terms. I wasn't
and there was nothing to suggest I was. But sometimes it
seems that people take what they want from your words
and make them fit their purpose. At the time, I was thinking of the way people looked at me in the street – I'd had
people making faces and twirling their hands round the
side of their faces in a mocking manner to suggest they
thought I had mental health issues – and trying to explain
that I was burnt out and weary rather than suffering from
a long-term problem. I was probably wrong on both counts
and I apologise for that.

But it did seem that some in the media who had *presumed*

I was suffering from depression – and remember, nobody at the ECB ever said I was – were now angry that I was saying I wasn't. It almost seemed that depression was the only mental health condition that had gained a foothold in the public consciousness – I think we have Marcus Trescothick to thank for the problem gaining such under-standing – and that nothing else counted.

One man who seemed to understand what I was going through was Gary Kirsten. He sent me an incredible email that showed great insight and empathy. He wrote of the 'never-ending battle to keep your head above the water', of 'how we mask' our weaknesses in order to sur-vive, but that eventually that isn't helpful and we have to deal with our problems. He said he wanted to commend me on my decision to go public with what I had been experiencing.

It was a beautiful email and one that, in many ways, I appreciate more now than I did at the time. When I first read it, again through the prism of my own shame and guilt, I was embarrassed that this man I so admired had felt the need to reach out and help me. Now, with the ben-efit of hindsight, I see how extraordinarily perceptive and kind it was of him.

He wasn't the only player, or former player, to reach out to me in those weeks after arriving home from Brisbane. Marcus Trescothick, who has done so much to educate society about the dangers of depression, also got in touch and we chatted about a few of our shared expe-riences. He made it clear that I could call him any time and I appreciate that greatly. But as things developed, it became increasingly apparent that, whatever similarities we had with our experiences, there were also some key differences.

There were times it crossed my mind to claim I was suffering from depression. It seemed to be what the world wanted to hear. It seemed the only thing that people wanted to hear; that would make them relent and leave me alone. It seemed some people required a diagnosis or label to satisfy them that I wasn't making the whole thing up.

But I wasn't ever diagnosed with depression. And I don't think I suffered from it. No doubt there must be some crossover between burnout, anxiety, depression and trauma, but I was fine away from cricket and it was only cricket-related events that triggered my difficulties.

At times it seemed even the ECB wanted to push me towards that diagnosis. Despite having only seen me a couple of times, Nick Peirce, the ECB's chief medical officer, called and told me he was going to drop off some antidepressants at my house. I have no idea why. It went against every other bit of advice I was ever given by Mark Wotherspoon, the England team doctor, and the psychologist the ECB were paying for me to see.

Might the ECB have been reluctant to embrace the idea that burnout was a factor? They might have feared that to do so would be to accept some of the blame; that it would have been interpreted as agreeing that the international schedule – bursting at the seams as it is – had contributed to my troubles. It was never my attempt to blame them or claim compensation or anything like that.

I'd be the first to admit I had some pre-existing fault

lines in my psychological make-up, and I'm not seeking to blame anyone for what happened. I don't blame the ECB at all and I am, generally, hugely grateful for the opportunities they gave me and the manner in which they tried to help when it all went wrong.

The setback in Cape Town occurred as the Sky interview was being aired and just ahead of the English county season. It meant I returned to Warwickshire with my confidence shot and no longer feeling any benefits from the break I'd had from the game. I already knew, deep down, that all the brave talk in the Sky interview, all my hopes for a quick recovery, were hollow.

To make matters worse, I turned up for the warm-up game against Gloucestershire at Edgbaston to find several TV crews and a posse of journalists in attendance. That never happens at county warm-up games and I knew they were there for a look at me. It was probably unreasonable of me to expect to recover away from the public eye – the scrutiny comes with the territory of being paid to play sport – but the level of interest definitely heightened my tension.

One of the journalists – again, from the *Telegraph* – was doing a 'Trott Watch' on Twitter. If I moved from mid-wicket to square leg, he would inform his followers. If I thick-edged one to third man, he made sure everyone knew. Maybe it was meant to be funny, but it felt as if my every move was being scrutinised, as if a few people were delighting in my misfortune. You learn who your friends are in such situations and some people were clearly just waiting for an opportunity to strike.

Since all this has happened, I've met a few people in different walks of life who have experienced similar troubles. The barrister who could no longer face standing up in court; the salesman who had lost the confidence to pick up the phone; the businessman who couldn't get out of bed; the doctor whose ability to make life-changing decisions under pressure had suddenly turned into an inability to cope with decisions as mundane as choosing between coffee and tea. Weary and broken people, from all walks of life, who had driven themselves to the brink.

With the benefit of hindsight, I can see that stress and anxiety can strike at just about anyone. If there was any difference between them and me – and I'd be the first to accept that most of them had far more important jobs than playing cricket – it was that they probably didn't go back to work with TV cameras scrutinising their every move. They don't wake up to another piece from Michael Vaughan suggesting you are 'conning' people.

Andy Flower came for a chat before play one morning. Andy can be hard and uncompromising – those qualities are strengths much of the time – but he was very supportive of me through this whole episode. He told me that there were many more important things in life than cricket and spoke in a way which suggested he had experienced similar troubles at times in his career. It reminded me of what a great guy he was when he let his guard down and made me wish he had felt able to do it a little more often during the period when he was coach.

In one of those warm-up games, I was trying to clip a full ball through the leg side and somehow only managed to make contact with it off the back of my bat. The ball scooped up behind me and found its way to fine leg. It was reported by some as a comparable dismissal to Brisbane, when I had been out pulling to a fielder in a similar position. It was a classic case of not allowing the facts to get in the way of a good story.

There were times when the expectation of playing for Warwickshire seemed higher than the expectation of playing for England. When you play international cricket, there is an acceptance that the quality of bowling is very high. So if you average 50 at that level and then go back to county level, it seems you are expected to score 50, at least, or you are letting your team down. It's an unhealthy way of thinking, of course, but it was something I was aware of often.

It all meant I went into the opening Championship match of the season at Edgbaston with my confidence low. To make matters worse, we elected to bat first on a damp pitch offering Sussex's seam attack – which included England seamer Chris Jordan and Australian Steve Magoffin – plenty of assistance. Somehow, though, something clicked: for whatever reason, I found myself able to focus on the ball and stay in the moment in a way I hadn't managed for many months. With the ball moving sharply off the seam, it was a little reminiscent of batting against the Pakistan seamers at Lord's four years previously. It was a tough challenge but I found myself enjoying it.

You wouldn't have guessed from the scoreboard. We were bowled out in the first session of the match for just 87 and, though I was frustrated to play on, I had made 37 of them in tough conditions and was eighth man out when left with the tail. It felt like a significant step forward. Tim Ambrose, with 20, was the only other man to make double figures and the next highest score was 4.

It wasn't to last. Standing at slip to the off-spin of Jeetan Patel, I put down a relatively straightforward chance offered by Ed Joyce in the slips and he went on to make a match-defining century. Nobody else in the Sussex side made more than 24.

I was distraught. I've always hugely valued playing for Warwickshire – Ashley Giles tells a story of me saying 'I don't care about the money' in a contract meeting – and it felt awful to let the side down. I was a senior player and was meant to set the tone for the less experienced guys to follow. But, as I saw it, I was the weak link who was costing us games.

By the time I batted in our second innings, I was a mess. I decided to go down swinging and was soon caught at deep backward square attempting a pull shot off Chris Jordan. Before then, though, I had been struck on the helmet by a bouncer from Magoffin and felt that all my faults and failings had been laid bare once more.

There's something about being troubled by a bouncer that hurts beyond the physical. It shines a light on the core of a batsman. It's not just that you have been beaten by a good ball – such as when you edge to the keeper – it's that you have, in many minds anyway, had your courage questioned. It's not your technique that is examined in such circumstances, it is your heart and bravery. It humiliates and degrades in a way that is hard to take for a man who once took pride in his ability to defy the fastest bowlers in the world. It felt like public humiliation.

To make matters worse, I dropped more catches in the second innings. I dropped Joyce again – twice, actually – and he went on to make another hundred. Belly – Ian Bell – had done exactly what a senior player should and clawed our way back into contention with a century of the highest class and I had let us all down by failing to hold on to relatively simple chances. I felt as if I had cost my team the match.

Some players – though not many, in my experience – go back to county cricket with a view that it is little more than an opportunity for practice between international fixtures. But it has never been that way for me. I have huge pride in representing Warwickshire and I care deeply about their success. The club has been a huge part of my life and it will always feel like home to me. My wife's grandfather, 'Tom' Dollery, had been a former captain of the club and had a bar named after him at the ground. The club was part of our lives in a way that extended far beyond the professional.

To let them down in this way was more than I could stand. I felt I was holding them back and knew I had to get away from the game. Before the end, I had decided to quit for good.

I called my agent, James, and asked him to speak to the ECB for me. 'I can't take this hurt any more,' I told him. 'Just tell them I quit. I can't face talking to them. Just tell them: no more.'

I meant it, too. Fortunately, though, James didn't make

that call. I was persuaded to make no hard decisions in the heat of the moment. But I went home pretty certain both that I would never be able to put myself through that trauma again and that there was no solution to my problems. Despite all the time off, despite all the help from the psychologist, I was no better than I had been in Brisbane. The same things kept happening and I had no idea how to stop them.

Over the next few days, James took a call from a friend of his who worked for the *Daily Mail*. Matt Lawton was a journalist who had interviewed several other sports people who needed help at some stage of their careers, notably Ronnie O'Sullivan and Steven Gerrard. Both of them had sought the help of the psychiatrist Steve Peters and gone on to find ways of dealing with their issues. Steve had also worked with Liverpool FC, the England football team and UK Athletics ahead of their excellent performance at the 2012 Olympics. Sir Dave Brailsford, performance director of British Cycling, referred to him as 'the best appointment I've ever made'. Matt subsequently interviewed Steve, found him highly impressive and passed on his details to James with the recommendation that I give him a call.

I called Steve, left a message on his answerphone and left the house to go shopping with Abi. We were heading to the Bull Ring and were just about to reach Five Ways roundabout in central Birmingham when he called back.

'I'd been expecting your call,' he said. 'I have a spot free this afternoon if you can make it?'

I drove back round Five Ways and headed up to see him. I had nothing to lose.

5

THE PEAK DISTRICT, MAY 2014

The road to recovery, for me, was the A520. That was the road that took me into the Peak District and to the home of Steve Peters.

It was, in every way, new territory for me. I had never visited the Peak District before – why would I? They don't play first-class cricket there – so I had no idea how beautiful and unspoilt the countryside remained. And, at the same time, I had never met anyone like Steve before.

Seeing him was my last throw of the dice. I had all but given up any hope of playing again, so I went into the process open-minded and prepared to try anything he suggested. It felt as if I'd tried everything else.

Steve didn't know much about cricket. In that first meeting, he referred to the pitch as 'the cricket green'. But that didn't matter. He knew a lot about sport – he is a pretty decent athlete himself and has set Masters records as a sprinter – and he had worked with many well-known sports people: Sir Chris Hoy credits him with winning Olympic gold in Athens in 2004; Sir Dave Brailsford hails him as 'a genius'; Victoria Pendleton and Ronnie O'Sullivan have said they would not have realised their potential without him; and Steven Gerrard was good enough to insist I give him a ring for a chat about his own experience.

I could hardly be anything less than impressed by such endorsements. While we all had different histories and issues, there was a common theme that united nearly all of us, whether performing in cycling, snooker, football or cricket. At some stage we had all allowed our thoughts to entangle and ensnare us. We had all struggled to fulfil our potential or had allowed our thoughts to become counterproductive.

Within minutes of my arrival, I knew Steve was going to help. I felt something I had not felt for a while: hope. He spoke with the insight of someone who understood and the confidence of someone who knew the solution. Within ninety minutes of the first session I felt the clouds of confusion clear and the burden of pressure lift.

'You're going to be fine,' he told me on that first day. 'It clearly isn't depression you've been suffering from. You are suffering from situation-based anxiety.'

I called Abi on my way home after that visit. 'I'm going to be fine now,' I told her.

I know that probably sounds naive. And I know I had felt optimistic before. It may even sound as if I were still in a state of denial as to the extent of my problems and looking to fool myself that a quick solution could magically help me recover my former powers of concentration and level of performance.

But this really did feel different. It really did feel as if Steve understood and, with his track record with sports people and his confidence in his method, it felt as if the storm was passing. By and large it was, too.

The diagnosis felt important. If you know what you are battling, you have a much better chance of defeating it, I reasoned, and Steve had offered clarity and, by doing so, reassurance. By telling me what I was suffering from and providing a programme for recovery, Steve was giving me something I could understand and could work at to help me overcome. I was flooded with relief. I now had a direction to go in.

And, yes, there was some relief that he didn't think I was suffering from depression. From what I knew at the time – and I accept that I was hugely lacking in awareness – depression was, in many ways, an irrational problem that could strike at any time and, as a consequence, didn't come with any obvious 'cure'. Naively, I thought that this alternative diagnosis of 'situational anxiety' might mean a more straightforward solution. And being able to give the illness a name suggested a game plan for recovery. I wanted to tackle this in same way I tackled challenges on the pitch. It felt more like a journey which I could complete with time and hard work.

I bought a copy of Steve's book, *The Chimp Paradox*. It blew me away with its insight and accuracy. It felt as if he were writing about me. At last someone understood. 'It's like he knows me,' I kept saying to Abi as I read it. 'It's like he's writing about me.'

For the first time in a while, I felt normal. My behaviour had an explanation. I wasn't the only one struggling with pressure and responsibility. I wasn't the only one suffering with this anxiety. For the first time in months, I didn't feel alone. Psychologists describe this as 'validation', I think. I can see that.

Over the next few weeks, I became a regular visitor to Steve's place. Eventually, even the drive up to see him became calming. Giving myself the time to appreciate the qualities of the countryside was, I'm sure, beneficial. Comforting and familiar. At times when either one of us was unavailable, I would talk to him by Skype.

'I'm not really looking at you as a person,' he told me. 'I see a machine that needs fixing.'

I could relate to that imagery. And I liked the idea that there was something akin to a repair manual that we could follow as it hinted at a complete fix. Had he talked about therapy and dialogue, I would have thought – on some level, at least – that I was in for a long haul; that there was no obvious solution; that it was a bit wishy-washy and rubbish.

But I could understand that machines break down. And I could understand that there are steps you take to mend them and that they require maintenance in the same way that the body requires exercise and healthy food. It all made sense.

The whole experience suddenly seemed more manage-able, less shameful – and yes, I know that is not a healthy way to have seen things – and, most of all, more hopeful. I could, at last, start to understand what was happening and explain it to those around me.

I suppose I had always had quite a literal mind growing up. I remember reading about Winston Churchill suffering from what he referred to as 'the black dog'. 'The black dog is upon me again,' he would write. Or 'The black dog is plaguing me again.' That sort of thing.

I now know he was using it to symbolise his depression. But, at the time, I had an image of an actual dog – a Hound of the Baskervilles-type creature – running around Downing Street, humping his leg, distracting him from his work and generally causing chaos. I wondered why a man so powerful couldn't ensure the dog was kept in a kennel or properly trained. I bet Hitler didn't have to deal with that sort of thing.

So I was quite happy when Steve began to explain the mind-management system detailed in *The Chimp Paradox*. In short, he suggests a working model that defines the human brain as a system with seven key parts. The ones which affect our thoughts, feelings and behaviour most powerfully are referred to in his model as the Human, the Chimp and the Computer. He suggests that there are two sides to a personality: the rational side, which he refers to as the Human, and the Chimp, which is the emotional and less rational side. While the Human side is responsible for your planning, your logical thinking and reasoning, the Chimp is responsible for your impulsive or emotional reactions, your initial feelings and many of your fears.

The Computer is where we store memories and information. It takes charge when we behave on automatic pilot. The Chimp and the Human can disagree about who takes charge of the Computer and this causes 'inner turmoil'. That is what I understand seemed to be happening to me when I was experiencing situation-based anxiety. My Chimp and my Human were battling. And my Chimp was winning.

As Steve explained his model to me, I found myself nodding my head in recognition of the characteristic he was describing. He talked, for example, of the Chimp catastrophising a situation, which was a classic mistake of mine. So, if I was in the nets, I feared I might edge one off a net bowler, all my teammates would see, the coaches would talk about it and drop me from the side. Before long, I'd be jobless and humiliated. Ridiculous, over the top thoughts. But absolutely the sort of mindset I had fallen into by that stage. My Chimp, as Steve explained it, was worried about losing his place in the troop. His ego was threatened by losing face and being seen as a failure.

My Chimp also controlled my anger, my anxiety and all those other self-defeating emotions that were bending me out of shape.

A couple of sessions in – as he understood the extent to which I was defined by my success or failure on the pitch – he exhaled and said: 'It's quite a big chimp that you're dealing with in there.'

'It's a silverback gorilla,' I replied.

And it was. The more I learned, the more I understood how I had been governed by my Chimp. How I had let basic fears dominate ahead of reason and how I had let those fears grow unchecked as I didn't know how to combat them.

Steve provided me with what you might describe as a formula. It wasn't just about applying it when times were tough, it was about changing the way I thought by controlling the Chimp and ensuring my rational brain dominated my decision-making.

The key phrase, for me, was to remember: I am an adult. I can handle anything that comes my way and I can control my emotions. At other times, I had to tell myself: I'm over-reacting.

There are three 'guarantees' at the heart of Steve's system. If you remember them, it prepares you for the disappointments that are inevitable and helps you remain on an even keel whatever life may throw at you. The first is that life isn't fair. The second is that the goalposts will always move. And the third is that there *are* no guarantees. Knowing the guarantees would help me control my Chimp, help me not to see life in such a black and white way and retain a sense of calm and control.

Little by little, I started to be able to predict how Steve would answer my statements. And, once I did that, I realised that I had understood his system and had the tools to cope with a comeback to cricket. I had Steve's voice in my head. I heard him remind me how to control my Chimp and understand the Chimp v Human struggles that had seen my performance deteriorate.

Gradually my focus started to change. For example, driving into Edgbaston had become an ordeal. Each time

I reached the barriers, I could feel myself sweating and my heart starting to pound. Steve suggested that, rather than avoid going to the ground until I could face it, I should return often, but with a different agenda.

So, in the period I was out of the team, I would take my daughter, Lily, on to the pitch in the intervals and throw a few balls for her so she could have a whack with her miniature bat. I knew people were watching me – even at county games, there were media and spectators who noted that I was back among the squad – but, as my attention was directed not on my performance but Lily's enjoyment, it was pressure-free. It helped me readjust my feelings towards Edgbaston not as a place of pressure and failure, but as a place where my daughter had a great time. It made returning more manageable and reminded me that cricket wasn't just about making a living, but about having fun.

I think it helped to remind myself of the other part of my identity, too. My identity as a father. It's a role that carries its own pressures and responsibilities, of course, but generally it's a role I have hugely enjoyed and at which I think I have been pretty successful. It's also a secure role: no one is ever going to 'drop' you as a father; only in extreme cases would people judge you in the media on your parenting. When you see your kids smiling and laughing, you receive immediate feedback and validation. Life seems simple and selfless and good.

For many years Edgbaston had been my home. I had lost it for a while when it was connected with failure and pressure and shame. But, thanks to Steve's advice, I felt I had it back. It wasn't just the place I played my cricket: it was the place I'd met my wife, a place my daughter loved to visit. It was relevant to all parts of my character, not just the cricketer.

I didn't only apply Steve's principles to cricket, either. If someone was driving slowly in front of me, or if my bank card was swallowed by an ATM, I called on Steve's words, controlled my emotions and reacted like an adult rather than a chimp. Most of the time, anyway. It felt as if I had a manual for living and I wanted to apply it to all areas of my life.

It was meant to be my benefit season. For those who don't know too much about county cricket, I should explain that there is a long-standing tradition where a county can grant a benefit season as reward to a long-serving loyal player once in his career. Typically, the player might host a series of dinners over the course of the season and there might be a couple of collections at well-attended county games. The Inland Revenue has traditionally granted tax breaks on the income from benefit seasons, with players sometimes earning well in excess of £100,000. It was, traditionally, a chance for players to earn enough money to set themselves up in retirement once their on-field career was over. In the old days, it might help a retired player buy a pub or a shop to ensure they were financially OK for the rest of their working lives.

I already had my doubts over how appropriate it was for me to have a benefit. While it was a huge honour – and deeply appreciated – I was never going to be comfortable effectively asking people for money when I had been on a highly paid central contract for several years. The idea that

I could host dinners or sell raffle tickets became entirely
inappropriate once I had taken that second break from the
game after the Sussex match. My benefit season effectively
didn't happen and I didn't lose a second's sleep over it.
Money is a wonderfully useful side-product of playing this
great game, but it never motivated or worried me.

Meanwhile, Mark Bawden, who was in contact with
Steve, and Graham Gooch put together a step-by-step process designed to ease me back into the game. The aim was
to start with low-pressure situations and incrementally
increase the amount of stress until they felt I was ready
for more.

So I started by training with the second team at
Warwickshire. That led to me playing for the second team
and, from there, training with the first team before making
a first-team return.

The first game was against Yorkshire 2nd XI at Stamford
Bridge. I was a little nervous, but we bowled first and I
picked up three wickets and then, when I was 12 not out,
it rained and there was no further play. It was, in many
ways, the perfect, gentle reintroduction I required: positive
but brief and not too demanding.

Playing second-eleven cricket had, in the past, felt like
a no-win situation for me. If I scored heavily, I was just
filling my boots against kids – and I was old enough to
be the dad of some of these guys – but if I failed it was
an embarrassment. A former world player of the year,
reduced to being bowled by a seventeen-year-old.

But that was part of the challenge now. I had to control
my ego rather than allowing the Chimp to control it. So I

saw every setback as part of my recovery. I wanted to be tested, and putting myself in situations where I could be shown up or humiliated was all part of that. I wanted to prove I could control my Chimp.

The next game was in Coventry, against a Durham 2nd XI that included Ben Stokes. I made an unbeaten 138 in the second innings, which did my confidence no harm at all, and followed it with an innings of 70 in a further game against Yorkshire 2nd XI in Pudsey, with nobody else in the side reaching 30.

That resulted in an early recall to the first team. I was a bit surprised by the choice of game – a televised T20 match at Northants – but I had decided not to look for any excuses, so I agreed to play and got on with it.

It didn't go great. We won, but I only made 1 and, after the next game at New Road, where I made a run-a-ball 39 and we lost, I was dropped. It was a setback and it did surprise me that, after all the talk of managing my return, I'd played in two relatively high-profile matches and was dropped for not being up to speed immediately. It didn't feel like it was what I needed at the time. But I was able to accept it as another test and went back to the second team determined to improve.

The next match was against Worcestershire seconds at Barnt Green. As we were warming up before the start, I heard Steve 'Bumpy' Rhodes – Worcestershire's director of cricket – telling his young keeper, Joe Clarke, to get inside my head when he saw me marking my guard.

Clarke, to his credit, didn't say a word. 'Listen to your own voice,' I told him while I was out there. 'No one else's.'

He smiled. I was out there a while, too, in making another hundred. It was a flat wicket, but it wasn't the worst attack and I felt pretty good. I felt in control.

In truth, playing in the seconds was fine. I didn't have a bad word directed at me and I saw a lot of talented young cricketers. I felt myself conquering the Chimp part of my personality – the part that tried to tell me I was in a no-win situation – and gain some rhythm and focus in my cricket.

All the while, Graham Gooch was making the journey to Edgbaston for sessions with me and Ian Bell. Within a few weeks, Gooch was firing new balls at me from close range trying to hurt me. It was brutal. But I found myself enjoying the challenge and enjoying the increasing confidence of knowing I could handle it.

A couple of times, Gooch would surprise me. 'You've edged that one, Trotty,' he said as I swayed out of the way of one lifter. 'No, I haven't,' I replied. 'My hands were nowhere near it.'

'Yup, you were out there,' he said.

'What the hell are you talking about, Goochy?' I said, starting to get angry that he was diminishing all the improvements I was making.

But then it hit me. He was testing me. He was putting me in the sort of position I might find myself in on the pitch: given out incorrectly. He was seeing how I handled it. Physically and mentally he was attempting to put me under stress to see how I reacted. He had given my Chimp a flick on the forehead and, just for a second, it wanted to jump up and beat its chest again. It was a good reminder.

I must give a word of thanks to the ECB at this stage. I

never even found out how much Steve charged: the ECB took care of everything. And Gooch, who was a freelance batting coach by that stage, never mentioned payment. It was all covered by the ECB. Apart from a couple of people, the vast majority were hugely supportive. I'm very grateful for that.

There had been a period when I felt forgotten by the ECB. It may be that they didn't want to burden me during my recovery – I'm sure that is the case with many people – but at times I felt as if I'd been consigned to the scrap heap. The ECB's chief medical officer, Dr Nick Peirce, visited only a couple of times in the six months following my return from Brisbane – and the managing director of England cricket, Paul Downton, only visited once. Prior to that, he had sent me the odd text to offer support. The words were right, but it felt perfunctory. However, the day after his visit, he happened to be interviewed by the BBC. When asked about me, he was able to say he had seen me the previous day. I wondered if he had only visited me so that he could say that he had.

After I announced that I was taking a further break from the game in April 2014 a piece appeared on ESPNcricinfo which suggested I was feeling cut off by the ECB. They weren't entirely my views and I hadn't any intention of criticising the ECB, but it did bring an interesting reaction. Within days, several other news organisations reported that I had failed to keep appointments with my psychologist and that I had ignored the ECB's demands when giving interviews a few weeks earlier.

Neither suggestion was true. I never missed an

appointment and, while it is true the ECB had some doubts about the interviews, they could simply have forbidden me, as a contracted player, to do them. They understood that I felt the need to talk to the media to correct some of the misinformation that was circulating.

A little digging made it clear that an individual within the organisation was leaking such information to the media to discredit me. I consider it the actions of a rogue employee and not reflective of the attitude of the ECB as a whole.

If I had a criticism – or some advice – it would be that the ECB should be looking to use Steve (or someone with his range of skills) on a more regular basis. Rather than calling on him only in times of crisis, it might well help sustain success if he was on hand at all times. He has a lot to offer.

My County Championship return came against Nottinghamshire. We won the game and I took a catch and a wicket with the ball but, in the second innings, I was out – caught at short leg – off a bouncer from Peter Siddle, a member of the Australian attack in that Brisbane Test, who was now with Notts as their overseas player. Bearing in mind everything that had happened previously, it was a dismissal that clearly brought back doubts – not least in my own mind – about my ability to cut it at that level.

But, once again, I implemented Steve's training and chose to interpret it as another test I had to pass on the road to recovery. I went out to celebrate with the rest of the team at the end of the match – in the past I might well have hidden myself away and fretted about the dismissal – and told myself that this was one of the inevitable setbacks that

I was always going to run into on my return. The way I saw it, I had to practise being out, practise failing, practise dealing with my ego and emotions, before I could claim that any of the changes I had made were permanent. It wasn't a system to deal with failure as much as to help achieve success. But dealing with failure – letting it go and not allowing it to become an impediment to future progress – is part of that.

It was also inevitable that I would receive a barrage of bumpers upon my return. But that wasn't an entirely bad thing. Against Durham, for example, John Hastings must have bowled me thirty bouncers on a pitch that was doing plenty. Had he pitched it up, batting would have been really difficult. As it was, he wasted the new ball and, as conditions eased, I took advantage and made 76, while Sam Hain made a century.

Did I play the short ball differently? Not really. I just received more of them. I'd never been a big hooker – I didn't see it as a percentage shot for me – and I'd always tended to duck the bouncer. If people thought I was ducking more often, it might just be that I was receiving a lot more bouncers.

I made a century against Sussex, too – especially pleasing bearing in mind the way I had started the season against them – then another against Northants and another against Durham to end the season. In between times, I scored heavily in List A cricket – I was the highest England-qualified scorer in the Royal London One-Day Cup that season – including centuries against Durham and Nottinghamshire.

In some ways, it was easier than trying to return at the start of the season. Nobody thought I was trying to 'con' them this time and I was given the space to go about my business without the media scrutiny I'd been under a few months previously.

There was the odd comment on the pitch and occasionally something from supporters. As I left Grace Road one day – I had been working there as an analyst for Sky – a group of drunken lads started jeering and making faces at me: twirling their hands round the side of their faces to suggest I was insane. Just for a second, my Chimp took over: it crossed my mind to turn around and confront them. But then I remembered I could just ignore the situation and I simply went home. It felt empowering to have gained such self-control – albeit maybe later in life than some – and it still provides me with greater confidence in all areas of my life.

Sometimes I struggled with it. Right before going into bat at Lord's one day, I had a pretty fierce row with my Warwickshire teammate Keith Barker. I hardly even recall what it was about, but I do remember being livid that, right before I went out to play, he was disturbing my concentration with some petty nonsense. I was so angry that, almost as soon as I took guard, I clubbed a ball to mid-on and was dismissed without scoring.

The match soon petered out into a draw but I was fuming. All the way home, I was fuming. Taking my kit out of the car I was fuming, explaining what had happened to Abi I was fuming. I could hardly sleep. The Chimp had been woken.

We were playing Kent in the semi-final of the Royal London One-Day Cup back at Edgbaston the following day. It was an important game for the club and I really wanted to contribute. But I was so angry I didn't think to check my phone, so I missed a message from the club's cricket operations manager, Keith Cook, informing me of a batsmen's meeting in the morning. I failed to make it.

But eventually Steve's words forced their way back into my mind. I realised that my anger wasn't helping the situation and that I had the power to control my emotions and take steps to make amends. I remembered that I was an adult and that I was over-reacting.

Before the game, we went into a huddle on the pitch. I could tell my mood had cast a shadow over the team, so I took the opportunity to tell them I had something to say. I apologised for my grumpiness the previous day, I apologised for over-reacting to a minor disagreement and I apologised for not making the meeting earlier.

The benefits were not just personal. As well as feeling my own anger subside as I talked, I could see the cloud of anxiety lift from my teammates. They were worried I was going to be a grumpy prick all day and that the atmosphere in the dressing room was going to be tense. My apology allowed us all to concentrate on the game without any baggage. I went on to make 58 – the highest score of the game – and play a part in us reaching the competition's final back at Lord's.

I also went back to using some methods I had, for some reason, abandoned along the way. I'd first started using the hypnotherapist Tammy Gooding after I pulled out of the Performance Squad at the end of 2008. Tammy is a broadcaster in the Midlands – she is currently with BBC Hereford and Worcester – and Abi and I got to know her after she was used as the on-field MC for some games at Edgbaston. We both liked her very much and were interested when we discovered she had branched out into hypnotherapy.

Anyway, back in 2008, after we had some sessions talking, she recorded me some messages which I put on my iPod or phone and listened to over and over again. The combination of her calming tones – she really does have a great voice for broadcasting – and the supportive messages helped me to both relax and to focus when the games started. I would listen to the same track over and over on bus rides in India or flights in Australia. I might listen in my hotel room at the end of a day or on the way to training in the morning.

They were simple things, really. Against a musical background – the gentle sort of neutral music you might find in a lift or dentist's waiting room – she spoke about watching the ball, about playing straight and about concentrating. There wasn't much talk about cricket, really, it was more about relaxing and feeling confident. She was, I suppose, talking to my subconscious as much as my conscious mind and I found that, after I listened to her words, I was in a good frame of mind to play. Concentrating on my role and blocking out the distractions seemed relatively straightforward.

Looking back now, it's frustrating that I stopped using the recordings. They did become quite monotonous – I must have listened to the same hour-long track about a thousand times – and I suppose I felt I didn't need them any more. But they were hugely helpful and, once I went back to using them in 2014, I started to enjoy more success again. It was stupid to stop using them. You live and learn. I have a lot to thank Tammy for – she really was instrumental in my international success.

It was only right at the end of the season that playing for England again ever entered my mind. It wasn't just that I didn't think they would ever pick me again – my place had gone to Yorkshire's Zimbabwean-born left-hander Gary Ballance, who had done a great job of taking his opportunity – it was that I didn't even want to think about putting myself in that situation.

But, after making a century against a strong Durham attack – Varun Aaron and Mark Wood bowled quickly and Chris Rushworth tested my technique – on a decent, Test-quality pitch at Edgbaston in the last game of the season, it did cross my mind that I was pretty much back to my best. I was scoring runs in both formats of the game on a consistent basis and I was coping with the inevitable setbacks that occur along the way.

So when Andy Flower phoned and asked me if I would think about going on the Lions tour, I gave him a bit of a silly – Chimp-dominated – answer. 'The Lions tour?' I answered. 'Surely you know what I can do by now?'

Andy was patient with me, though, and explained that it was the next step in my recovery. He also invited me on what was, ostensibly, a fast bowlers' training camp to Potchefstroom before Christmas.

I thought about it for a few hours, but I had to say yes, didn't I? It was fun, too. The fast bowlers present included Stuart Broad, Jimmy Anderson, Matt Dunn, Boyd Rankin and Mark Wood and it soon became apparent that part of the purpose of me being there was to see how I reacted when they peppered me in the nets. It went very well and was another good test of my recovery.

It went well off the pitch, too. We had a meeting the first night I arrived – of course we did; the ECB love a meeting – and I was able to open up about my experiences with anxiety over recent months. Again, you could feel there was some apprehension from my fellow players about how to broach the issue, so it was healthy to clear the air. There were a couple of very talented young batsmen there, too – Gary Ballance and Hampshire's James Vince – who I knew would have their own experiences with similar pressures. If I could help them relieve some of that pressure, I would be delighted. They are the future now and I'll take a lot of pleasure from watching them excel.

A few weeks before the Lions tour, Andy called again and asked if I fancied taking on the captaincy. I thought about it for a day or two as I was concerned I didn't need the added burden but, in the end, I said yes with some gratitude. I figured it wouldn't do any harm at all to focus on the fortunes of the whole team rather than just my own game – there would simply be less time to obsess on my own issues – and I knew this was another attempt to test me by gradually increasing the pressure once more. It was another step on the journey back to the England team and it was an honour.

Lions tours are always slightly tricky. Whereas the emphasis on a senior tour is on winning, the emphasis on a Lions tour is on impressing enough to win a chance to go on a senior tour. So while you want to improve your own game and demonstrate that you are a good team player, you are also hoping to do a bit better than other people on the trip. The dynamic therefore is inevitably more about individual success than is ideal in a team game.

It's also inevitable that you are going to feel as if you are on trial on these tours. You are. You are being scrutinised to see not just how you perform on the pitch, but how you mix with your colleagues off it and how you will react to being thrown together for weeks on end with people you may not know very well.

The tour didn't start particularly well from a personal perspective. After the first innings, when I was out for 6 after the openers, Adam Lyth and Sam Robson, both made centuries and number three Alex Lees made 85, I could feel many of the old anxieties return. A Skype call to Steve reminded me that this wasn't life or death and, in the second innings, I made an undefeated 79 to gain some confidence. In truth, though, the opposition – a Gauteng Invitation XI – was pretty modest and it was little more than a gentle warm-up. Those runs didn't mean much.

The next game was far more challenging and all but sealed my return to the England team. In conditions where the temperature never dropped below 35 degrees and against an attack only a fraction below Test class (it included Chris Morris, Ryan McLaren, Dane Piedt, Rory Kleinveldt and Beuran Hendricks), I made an unbeaten double hundred and spent all but ten overs of the match on the pitch.

There were several high-profile coaches on that tour. There was Andy Flower, who remained highly influential despite having stood down as head coach, there was Mark Robinson, who was in charge of the tour and was clearly – and quite rightly – very well thought of at the ECB, there was Ottis Gibson, the former West Indies coach who'd come back to the ECB to coach the bowlers, and Graham Thorpe, the lead batting coach at the ECB. I could feel the eyes of all of them upon me and I knew I had to convince them all.

I had to convince myself, too. I had to convince myself I could concentrate for long periods, that I still had the hunger and composure to cut it at the top level.

That moment came right at the end of day three. I had batted all day and earned a position where we had drawn even with the South Africans' first-innings total when I played a sweep off Piedt and ran four. To show that desire, concentration and fitness proved to everyone that I was batting at the sort of level that had gained my international selection in the first place. Robinson, who led a debrief at the end of the day, mentioned it in his team talk and congratulated me for leading from the front. I knew I had sent a message to the England selectors.

When I look back on that innings, it has parallels with the double century I made on my debut for Warwickshire's second team. On both occasions, I knew it was make or break. On both occasions, I knew that even a century might not be enough. I knew I had to make a massive score to answer all the doubts and make an irrefutable case for my selection. To score so heavily, to focus so well, under that pressure was hugely pleasing.

It was probably relevant that Lyth and Lees were both out for single-figure scores in that innings. Robson made 41 but, in the battle for a top-order place, I had gone to the front.

I was out for a duck in the first innings of the next 'Test' but made a half-century in the second innings (against an attack that now included South Africa's outstanding young fast bowler Kagiso Rabada) and none of my top-order colleagues – or rivals – were able to do any better. Robson, who is a player I rate highly, made 5 and 0 in that match, while Lees, who has a great future, made 5 and 9, and Lyth, who looked an elegant player, followed his first-innings 65 with a second innings of 37.

It wasn't for a couple of months that it was confirmed I would be in the squad to tour the Caribbean. James Whitaker, the head selector, had emailed a few times from Australia – where he was watching England's unhappy World Cup campaign – to say 'Well done' and arrange an end-of-tour debrief. But it was not until Warwickshire's pre-season tour to Barbados that Mick Newell, the Nottinghamshire director of cricket and another England selector, passed on the news to Dougie Brown, the director of cricket at Warwickshire, that I was going to be named in the party. Less than eighteen months after leaving the Ashes tour, I was back in the England squad.

Andy Flower:

It took great courage to come back into the Test side. Had he retired after he came home from Brisbane, he could have looked back with justifiable pride on an excellent career.

But he decided to fight back. He decided he didn't want to end his career that way and I think his love for the game convinced him to play on. He really wasn't a guy to take the easy decision at any stage. It is one of the qualities I most like in him. He deserves a lot of credit for that.

None of his rivals for the role – guys like Sam Robson – had done especially well on the Lions tour and he did have an excellent international record to support the argument that he was the man for the job. I think it's fair to say that Alastair Cook was a pretty strong supporter of his inclusion and wanted a senior player he knew and trusted at the other end. All of that was understandable.

But I did have a few doubts. He had scored a double hundred on a very flat pitch in Paarl during which he had never really been tested by the short ball. The pitch was just too slow.

6

AUSTRALIA, 2010–11
The Rise

It's a hot morning in Adelaide. Straussy has lost the toss, so we're in the field. The pitch looks a belter. If we don't strike with the new ball, this could be a tough day.

Jimmy Anderson is bowling the first over and Shane Watson is on strike. Watson is so strong playing down the ground, we tend to have a deep, straight mid-on and a straighter than normal mid-wicket. I'm the straight mid-wicket.

On this occasion – as so often with Watson – there's a lot of pad on the ball when he plays his stroke, so it just dribbles into the leg side. I keep my eye on the ball as I run towards it, so I don't know exactly where the batsmen are or who has hesitated, but I can hear their cries of anguish and the excitement of our fielders. I know there's been some sort of mix-up. I pick up, balance myself and know, even before I release the ball, that I'm going to hit despite only having one stump to aim at. Simon Katich is run out and, next ball, Ricky Ponting edges a perfect

*outswinger to slip. They are two down without scoring a run
and, after Ponting walks off cursing himself and his luck, we
know we have them rattled. We're going to win the Ashes.*

That was December 2010. When asked to reflect on the
high point of my career, it was the moment that came to
mind. The run-out was the culmination of so much work
on my fielding and confirmed, to me at least, that I was
able to contribute to the side beyond scoring runs.

It was more than that, though. At that moment, it felt as
if I was in a team that was going to the top. I had complete
confidence in my game and complete confidence in my
teammates' game. We were going places. We all knew it
and we were all loving it.

It was a great tour. We were always a bunch of individuals with our own ambitions and egos but, for a year or
two, we all bought into the team ethos. We all knew that
we needed each other to achieve the success we wanted.
We had shared goals and shared experience. We had come
through a lot together to reach that point.

There is another moment from that tour that sticks out.
Walking off at the end of the second day of the Melbourne
Test a few weeks later, I looked around to see an obviously
dispirited Australia side who had accepted the Ashes were
gone. They knew they were beaten.

They were right, too. They had been bowled out for
98 on the first day and, by the time play finished on day
two, we were 346 runs ahead with five wickets in hand.
We knew we were going to win and I was 141 not out –
meaning that, for the second Ashes series in succession, I

had scored a century in the match that sealed the result. It doesn't get much better than that.

It's only when I came to look back on my career that I realised that my period in the Test team coincided with its entire life cycle. Do not think for a moment that I'm claiming I was the reason we enjoyed such success – though I like to think I contributed – or that I'm claiming the team couldn't manage once I was gone. It's more that I can see now how fortunate I was to be in the right place at the right time and play alongside so many fine cricketers and coaches. And it all came together perfectly on that Ashes tour.

Andrew Strauss:

When I took over as captain, things were messy. The team had just been through the Kevin Pietersen and Peter Moores sackings and the Stanford thing had only just happened. You could feel that everyone wanted a fresh start.

Maybe that is why everyone bought into the new ideas so readily. Very early in our time together, we realised we had an unusually talented group of players and there was talk of developing into the best England team there had ever been. Some of the players – such as Kevin Pietersen – were already pretty well known, while others – such as the new-ball pairing of Jimmy Anderson and Stuart Broad – developed quickly in their new roles.

But then there were guys, such as Swanny and Trotty, who came from nowhere, really, to become key members of the side.

It was a combination of right time, right place in the
way we came together and we were driven pretty hard by
the goal of becoming number one in the world.

When I came into the set-up, at the end of the summer of
2009, our rebuilding phase was just beginning. The team
had been through some tough times. They had been beaten
by India and South Africa in the home Test series the previous two summers, had underperformed in two World T20
tournaments – losing at Lord's to Holland only a couple
of months earlier in one of them – and had been forced
through some uncomfortable moments by the Stanford
game and the sackings of Peter Moores and KP. Only a
few months earlier, they had lost to West Indies in the
Caribbean. Nobody, at that stage, was looking for any more
drama off the pitch. They just wanted to win some games.

Despite those modest results, though, there was remarkable confidence in the dressing room. You looked around
and you saw a strong opening pair, two skilful new-ball
bowlers, a fine spinner who could bowl in any conditions
and a couple of middle-order batsmen with great records.
We had all the ingredients and I was, I suppose, one of the
final pieces of the jigsaw.

In Andrew Strauss we had a great communicator who
had proved himself a fine batsman having come through
some tough moments a year or two earlier. As such, he
had the complete respect of everyone in the dressing
room – and I absolutely include KP in that – but he also
understood the negative thoughts that could drag a player
down if form or fortune was against them.

One of the most valuable qualities in a dressing room is calm. The last thing you want is an anxious captain or coach spreading their insecurity through the team. But with Straussy, you always had the impression that he was in control, that he had confidence in the team and that the situation was in hand.

Not everyone would have been able to cope with the combination of big personalities he had to manage. In that 2009 Ashes series, Strauss had Graeme Swann, KP and Andrew Flintoff in one dressing room at times. But it is a measure of his standing that each of them respected him and listened as attentively as the rest of us when he spoke. It was, very clearly, *his* team and he ensured everyone pulled together for the common good rather than allowing anyone to grandstand or coast.

You always felt Strauss backed you. Even after a bad day – maybe particularly after a bad day – you felt he was on your side. And because of that, you wanted to play not just for the team, but for him. He wasn't one to make speeches all the time or hold endless meetings – he disliked those as much as the rest of us – but when he spoke the dressing room was silent. He oozed common sense and calm. He was absolutely the sort of guy you would follow into battle.

Andy Flower was also excellent at that time. It took me a while to realise it, but he was quite different as a coach and a man. It was almost as if he felt he had to play a part as a coach; that he had to be controlled and cold and demanding. As a man, he is much warmer, more sympathetic and gentler than you might imagine.

He had been very close to Peter Moores and felt badly for him when he was sacked. It was probably hard for him to forgive KP for his part in that for a while, but he managed it. At the time I entered the dressing room, there were no obvious signs of tension between the two of them. Instead there was obvious mutual respect and an understanding that, by working together, we could achieve something special. It really was a case of the right people coming together at the right time in their careers.

One of Andy's qualities was his consistency. He never contradicted himself and never allowed anyone to think he could be persuaded or manipulated. That is an important quality for a coach; players soon sniff out any weakness or vulnerability and use it to their advantage. In time, it started to become perceived as stubbornness but, for a team at the start of a new era, it provided welcome parameters.

Many times he pushed me on. On, out of my comfort zone. On, beyond what I thought I could do. In my first senior tour, to South Africa in 2009, the ODIs preceded the Test series and I was desperate to break into the side. Andy held meetings with all the players over the first couple of days of the tour and told me I had a five out of five chance of making the Test team, but only a one out of five chance of playing in the ODIs.

I took that as a challenge. But, though I made 85 in the first warm-up game in Bloemfontein, I suffered with cramp towards the end of my innings and was out going for a slog knowing I couldn't run many more. Andy was unimpressed.

'You've ten days to sort yourself out,' he said to me afterwards, suggesting my fitness would have to improve markedly if I was to survive in international cricket. I was left out of the next game, but he insisted on running me ragged in the warm-up before it, hitting any number of tough catches and making me dash about until my lungs were bursting. He didn't stop until the umpires were half-way out to the middle. I took the point and I worked damn hard to improve my fitness and agility. I knew I had to if I was going to be selected.

It was tough, but it was also what I needed. I didn't resent the extra work he made me do. I appreciated that he thought I was worth the investment.

Even during the century I scored in the Melbourne Test that secured the Ashes, Andy found ways to push me on. I took a cracking blow to my left knee off an inside edge when I had scored about 80 off the bowling of Ben Hilfenhaus and struggled for a while afterwards. My knee ballooned to such an extent that, when the physio came on to have a look at it, I was unable to roll up my trousers and instead had to take them down. I took a couple of painkillers at the time, but forty minutes or so later, I could hardly move so I called for more help.

The twelfth man ran on with a couple of painkillers and a message from Andy. 'If you need a bullet to bite on, I have one up here,' he had said, the inference being that I should quit complaining and get on with it. I'll show the bastard who's tough, I thought to myself. Again he had found a way to motivate me. He knew which buttons to press.

Over time, that quality – that toughness – became less effective. It eroded our goodwill. He made me go out to bat after I had damaged my shoulder in the Trent Bridge Test against India in 2011 when I was nothing more than a punch bag for the bowlers. I couldn't play shots or evade the ball, and at times like that I recall thinking, 'Jesus, Andy, just lighten up for once; just be a bit flexible.' But it wasn't his way. And, for a while at least, it was highly effective.

One of the unsung heroes of our rise was the analyst, Nathan Leamon. The role of these analysts and the statistics they provide has come in for some criticism in recent times, but they can offer insight and they did play a part in our development in those years. Specifically, Nathan gave the team a presentation at the ECB's National Performance Centre in Loughborough just ahead of the South Africa tour of 2009–10. In it he detailed how we could rise to number one in the world rankings 'in a couple of years' and broke down exactly how it could happen. He went through series by series, noting the ranking points available depending on the results, and detailing how we could rise up the table with each success.

You could hear the murmurs of approval as Nathan spoke. He really captured the imagination of that group of players and you could feel people come together with a common goal at that very moment.

We were motivated in different ways. For most of us – and I put myself firmly in this category – the chance to play in the best side in the world was thrilling. It was what I had always wanted and to see, for the first time, a clear route by which it was possible was tantalising. I couldn't wait to get started.

For one or two others, the allure was also the fame and fortune that could accompany success. That is not a criticism; just an observation. There were significant financial bonuses on offer – more than £300,000 a year for a player involved in all formats – and that did become a topic of conversation for a few guys. Take the summer of 2013, for example: the bonus and prize money for winning the Champions Trophy was £2 million, with another £1 million for winning the Ashes. It's a lot of money, isn't it?

What Nathan offered was a route by which we could fulfil our ambitions: fame, fortune or the satisfaction of a job well done, the path was the same. We all wanted the same thing, even if it was for different reasons.

I never played for money. It's a lovely thing to come your way but honestly, if I can afford to buy the more expensive brand of peanut butter that I like, I'm happy. If that sounds ridiculous, it is because when I was growing up my mum always bought the cheaper brand and I never liked it as much. I used to look up at the nicer brand on the super-market shelf and think, 'One day you'll be mine.' Even now, I like to keep a pot of it in the house. Good peanut butter, for me, has always defined success. I never felt I needed much more.

I was always quite different to Kev that way. After the Adelaide Test of 2010, we talked of how we would cele-brate. I recall treating myself to a steam and massage in the hotel. He treated himself to hiring a Lamborghini.

It's fair to say KP and I had never really got on before I was picked for the Test side. I hadn't particularly rated him when we grew up – nobody had; well, nobody except him – and I think he saw me, a guy who had been fast-tracked into the South Africa U19 team, as someone to take down. He was fairly abrasive on the pitch – though that wasn't unusual – and there was always a bit of an edge when we came up against one another in a county game. I recall giving him a fearful send-off after I dismissed him in the C&G Trophy final at Lord's in 2005 after he attempted to hit me back to Cape Town and managed only to slog to the fielder on the boundary.

There wasn't much opportunity to get to know him during my brief spell in the England T20 team in 2007, so when he approached me after the Oval Test of 2009, I had just a little trepidation about what he was going to say. But he was great. He hobbled up with his leg in a cast having recently had an operation on his Achilles tendon, shook my hand and congratulated me on my century.

We never looked back. Even after we were involved in a run-out early in the first Test we played together – he pushed one into the covers and set off on a single; I leaned on my bat at the non-striker's end and watched him – we never fell out or exchanged a cross word.

Maybe it was the shared background, but I always found Kev a straightforward character. What is perceived as arrogant in England is seen as upfront and honest in South Africa and he needed that incredible self-belief to make him the player he has become. He is incapable of sugar-coating his opinions – a characteristic that can cause offence in England, where the culture is more subtle than South Africa – and that has created some issues, but he accepted me for who I was and I did the same to him.

You have to be tough to make it in the aggressive environment of South African age-group cricket and it was perhaps the case that Kev and I could seem a bit arrogant or belligerent in our attitudes. Even Matt Prior and Andrew Strauss, who were born in South Africa, could be surprised by Kev, but they had left at a much younger age and maybe didn't completely understand how abrasive a development we had. I wouldn't call it a culture clash exactly, but I do think we understood one another a little better because of our shared past.

Nobody could have predicted how good he would be if they'd seen him as a teenager in South Africa. He was a dodgy off-spinner who slogged it with the bat. I wouldn't have given him a prayer of playing Test cricket. Even after he started his limited-overs international career so well, I thought he would struggle in Test cricket as he didn't have the tight technique that I thought was required. But he broke the mould and proved me wrong. He kept proving me wrong. Eventually, in Mumbai in 2012, he played the best Test innings I have ever seen.

It takes incredible strength of mind to believe in yourself when the world doubts you. And it takes incredible strength of mind to continue to play in the manner you think suits you best when the world is full of criticism. But he counter-attacked during his first Test century – that Ashes-clinching effort at The Oval in 2005 – and he counter-attacked in Australia in 2013–14. Too often people forgot how much success he had enjoyed with his positive style when it didn't work out.

It was great to bat with him. Such was his reputation and physical stature at the crease that you could see the body language of the opposition change. Sides were so worried about him, it took the pressure off his batting partner. He had such power – I once saw him hit a ball over the OCS stand at The Oval in a net session – such confidence and such reach that he was almost impossible to subdue when the force was with him.

Beneath that exterior of huge self-confidence, though, Kev is just like the rest of us. He can be hurt, he can be insecure and he can suffer the same paranoia and concerns. He is hugely loyal to his friends and values time with his family above everything. I still feel the roots of the fall-out between him and some of our teammates were in poor communication and misunderstanding. He felt under-appreciated and they felt excluded. Tensions rose and divides deepened. It does seem there is no way back now but, from my experience, he couldn't have done more to support or try to help me.

With Kev and Cooky in the same side, we had two batsmen I would consider great. They complemented one another, too, in their wildly contrasting styles, Cooky blunting the attack and KP picking up the pace and giving our bowlers time to bowl the opposition out twice. Clearly there was more to it than that – when you have batsmen as good as Ian Bell in the side, it was certainly more than a two-man line-up – but that was the basic formula.

Alastair Cook:

When people talk about the qualities of that England side – the relentlessness, the reliability, the ability to grind our opposition down – they are talking about Trotty's qualities.

KP apart, there probably weren't any 'star' names in our side. But there were about thirteen of us who knew our games very well and managed to play incredibly consistent cricket over two or three years.

Trotty was an absolutely key figure. We wouldn't have become number one in the world without him. He had a huge appetite for batting and, if he reached 40, he nearly always went on to make a big hundred. He was almost impossible to get out. For several years, he drove us on to be the team we became. That century at the MCG was a brilliant, brilliant innings. He was a huge part of how we played. I hope people remember that.

It became obvious pretty quickly that we had a bit of a formula in the field, too. At the start of almost every session – first or second innings once the ball was about thirty overs old – we would throw the ball to Jimmy Anderson and Graeme Swann and expect them to strike for us.

Jimmy had started his career as an outright quick bowler. But after some setbacks, not least with injury, he settled into the highly skilled fast-medium bowler that we see today. He tended to get me out for fun when we played in county cricket and, though I felt I could pick which way he was going to swing it from the way he loads before delivery, playing it was another challenge entirely.

He seems to have developed this reputation for being dangerous only in English conditions. It's just rubbish. Anyone who watched him in Australia in 2010–11, India in 2012 or the UAE in either of his tours there, saw him bowl magnificently well in conditions that offered him almost nothing. The home team's captain M.S. Dhoni rated him 'the difference between the sides' in India, where he maintained an incredibly tight line and length and generated just enough reverse swing to take wickets. If you want to know how good he is, just ask any batsman: he's magnificent.

He is pretty quiet in the dressing room. He has played for a long time now and he knows what he needs to do in terms of his preparation and recovery and takes that stuff very seriously. Bearing in mind the amount of overs he has bowled for England – and for many years, he was the busiest international bowler in the world; an incredible achievement for a seamer – he is something of a miracle in terms of his longevity. He has remained very light, which I'm sure has enabled him to remain fit, and he has continued to pick up new skills. When I reflect upon how tough I found it to play 50 Tests, I am full of respect and admiration for his ability to keep going well past 100. England have leaned incredibly heavily on him for a long time.

Swanny was the best spinner I ever faced. I know that will surprise people, but he bowled a brilliant length which made it hard to know whether to go forward or back to him, and he did it at a pace which gave you little chance to readjust if you got it wrong. He changed his pace really well, while at the same time gaining a drift that meant he threatened you on both edges of the bat.

He used to laugh in the dressing room when they showed a split screen on TV of the variation between the ball that turned in and the ball that drifted away. More often than not, he relied on natural variation and was always honest about it. But if he didn't know which way the ball was going, what chance did the batsman have?

I admired Swanny in several ways. Despite that jovial image he cultivated in the media, he took his cricket very seriously. I played against him when he was at Northants and he was pretty average; he bowled some nice spells, but he would try to mix it up too much and you always felt you could get on top of him.

That all changed after Stephen Fleming, the former New Zealand captain, played with him as an overseas player at Nottinghamshire. Inspired by Fleming's advice and example, Swanny became a more disciplined, more focused cricketer. He finally understood that he had to take his talent seriously and realised what it took to make it at the top level. He became ruthless and reliable on the field but, off it, he hardly changed. He was still the same amusing, high-energy guy who had so annoyed coach Duncan Fletcher on his first England tour. We're very different people – I think we only exchanged mobile phone numbers after we finished playing together – but I admire Swanny for never changing as a man while improving his game out of recognition.

You need a guy like Swanny in the dressing room. Sure, he annoyed me a few times when I thought he took a joke a bit far but there were many more times when his humour defused the tension or re-energised a tired group of guys. Nobody should ever mistake that apparently casual demeanour for a lack of passion or strength: in the toughest moments, he was right there in the thick of the battle and by the time he retired, midway through the 2013–14 Ashes tour through injury, he had given his last drop for England. There was nothing left in that right elbow and I don't for a second blame him for retiring when he did. But I guess I would say that, wouldn't I?

I'm not sure anyone had as big an impact on the way we played as Swanny. He was so tight, even on pitches offering him nothing, that we could get away with a four-man attack and play six specialist batsmen and Matt Prior at number seven.

Matt was a huge part of our success, too. He was keeping for Sussex in the match where I scored a century for Warwickshire on debut, way back in 2003, and I remember thinking then that he could go a long way as a wicketkeeper-batsman. I was shocked to play against them next season and find that he was no longer keeping. It took him a while to realise how good he could be and understand how hard he would have to work to achieve it.

We had a bit in common in that regard. Like me, Matt had been a highly rated young player. And, like me, he had relied too much on that natural talent before realising how hard, and smart, you have to train if you're going to sustain a career at international level. By the time we played together, he had a terrific work ethic and had developed into – in my opinion – the best wicketkeeper-batsman England have ever had.

He didn't always get the respect he deserved for the way he played. His job, very often, was to accelerate us towards a declaration or towards the end of our innings. Sometimes left with the tail, often batting against the second new ball, he became a terrifically selfless cricketer who let a fair few personal milestones – half-centuries and centuries – slip by in the team cause. Those things win a lot of respect in the dressing room.

That work ethic was something else that united the squad. You couldn't come in to training and take it easy because the guy next to you would put you to shame with the work he was doing. We all spurred one another on as you didn't want to be the one to let anyone down. In terms of talent and hunger and experience, that team came together at the perfect time.

While some guys were inspired by individual goals, they were never helpful for me. I never thought, I must score 1200 runs this season, or, I must score two centuries and two half-centuries this series. That might work for some players, but for me it would have led to looking too far ahead. I was always better off concentrating on scoring the next five runs and leaving the future to look after itself.

But the motivation of rising up the world rankings, of winning the Ashes home and away, of becoming the best team in the world, unified us. And after Nathan broke it down for us and made it clear exactly what we had to do, we all understood how those goals could be achieved.

So, very early on, we realised we had an opportunity to do something special. Despite our lowly world rankings, there was talk that we could be the best. It could have sounded absurd – it's not as if our results justified such confidence – but we all believed it and, just as important, we were all prepared to work together to achieve it.

It wasn't easy to win acceptance in that dressing room, though. There was a group of guys who had played with each other for a while and known each other for longer. They had their own shared history, their own jokes and their own social group. That's fine. It's what you expect and it's natural.

But there were times this seemed exclusive. There were times it seemed as if they were all in on a joke at your expense. If you were a new player, a player who was out of form or just didn't fit in with the gang, it wasn't easy. It wouldn't help you relax and play your best cricket.

I was fortunate in that I scored runs early. That helped win acceptance and helped me feel as if I belonged. But I saw a few others come and go – Nick Compton was one, though he may yet prove me wrong – without ever truly being accepted. Maybe it isn't that simple. Maybe it's just that they felt they didn't win acceptance.

In my experience, pretty much everyone knows how hard international cricket is and there is always a will to see your new teammates succeed. But unless you hit the ground running, the negative thoughts can start to worm into your head and, with all the other players busy with their own challenges and tribulations, a new dressing room can seem a lonely place.

I clashed with the group in Bangladesh in 2010. I felt I was struggling to cement my place in the side and I had just been given out caught off the helmet – a ridiculous decision, really, with the ball going nowhere near the bat or the glove – and I came back to the dressing room feeling angry and uptight.

'Ball just brushed your glove, didn't it?' Swanny asked as I sat down.

'Nowhere near it,' I replied.

'Yeah, just brushed your glove,' he said. He probably meant no harm, it was just his way of lightening the mood and getting a laugh from his mates, but when you feel your place is in jeopardy and you could do with a bit of support, he wasn't always the most sensitive guy to be around.

I let that moment go, but I was beginning to simmer under the surface. The moment my temper came to the boil was during the second Test in Dhaka. The batsman had just clipped one off his legs to my left at deep backward square. It was always a single. I ran round, picked it up and threw it in without any drama. But then I saw Matt Prior having a laugh with Graeme Swann, at slip, and Paul Collingwood, at gully, mimicking a fielder who was back on his heels, suggesting – to my mind at least – that I hadn't been concentrating in the field.

I exploded. 'Don't fucking start that with me, Prior,' I yelled at him. 'I've had enough of your bullshit. It's hard enough without your own teammates taking the piss. I'm not taking this. It stops now.' I went on. And on. It probably only lasted thirty seconds, but it felt like an age at the time. The team were shell-shocked.

'What the hell is happening here?' Colly asked.

'Do you think what you're doing now is helping?' Graeme Swann shouted back.

'And you can fuck off, too, you prick,' I replied.

'You guys have had this coming,' KP shouted at them from mid-on. 'I told you this would happen.'

For a while the game seemed irrelevant as we fought among ourselves. The Bangladesh batsmen looked stunned.

Matt ran up to me at the end of the innings as I was running off to put my pads on to open the batting. 'Let's put all that behind us, mate,' he said.

'Fine,' I replied.

But in the dressing room Andy Flower was unimpressed. 'Something happened out there that doesn't happen on the field when we play,' he said. 'Trotty, I want you to apologise to the boys.'

I couldn't believe it. But, later that day, I went to each of their hotel rooms and apologised. Matt looked awkward as I mumbled sorry. But they didn't do it again and I'm not at all sure it wasn't a beneficial experience. I really don't think they were trying to make me feel uncomfortable or exclude me; it was more that they didn't realise how alienated a player could be in a new, pressurised environment; especially if they were struggling with their form.

Kevin Pietersen:

I had warned Andy Flower in Bangladesh that Trotty was at breaking point. The way he was being treated was horrendous. It was just a horrible environment. Some of the guys, thinking they were being funny or clever, were actually just making a sensitive guy who was trying to find his way in international cricket feel undermined.

If this sort of behaviour happened in an office or school it would be regarded as bullying. Flower seemed shocked and said he would send people home if he found it to be true. But nothing changed. I think that he allowed the atmosphere to fester because he thought we would push each other along that way. He never seemed to want it to become too cosy or comfortable. Trotty used to say he treated us like racehorses and that is exactly right: if we won we would get a sugar lump; if we lost we would be out in the field without any attention or care.

Trotty just snapped in Bangladesh. He had taken a lot of shit and he couldn't take any more. He was shouting and screaming at the guys. He was telling them to fuck off from the edge of the boundary and you could see it really rattled them.

I wanted to defend Trotty. I pulled Swann and Prior into the toilets and told them it had to stop. I told them that if they continued to behave like that, I would start to treat them the same way.

I didn't know until now that Trotty was the one who Flower made apologise even though he only snapped due to the others' behaviour. That's ridiculous. What sort of environment forces the bullied to apologise to the bully? Well, that's the England environment we were in at the time. It was poisonous.

Andy Flower:

I'd see the Bangladesh incident as part of the evolution of that team. It was the 'forming and storming' phase that is probably necessary and normal.

Trotty made it clear he wasn't going to take any of that crap and I was broadly OK with that. I had confidence that he could play and I saw it as part of the process of getting to know one another.

Earning peer respect is one of the biggest drivers in terms of improved performance and Trotty had already proved to himself – and shown everyone else – that he could play with that century on debut. But if you're spending a lot of time with people in dressing rooms, these things can happen as people learn to get on with one another. I didn't see that as a major issue.

I know Kev thought that the behaviour in the England dressing room amounted to bullying. That is a strong word, but I know what he meant. It wasn't exactly how I saw it. I viewed it more as a rite of passage; a period you had to go through while you earned your stripes. You might even describe it as 'tough love'. Test cricket is hard and this may have been the team's way of saying 'Toughen up; this is no playground.' But it wasn't helpful and it wasn't necessary. If you were under pressure or out of form, it added to the burden. I think it's improved a fair bit now.

That side of things definitely deteriorated, at least for a while, once Andrew Strauss stepped down. He was held in such respect in that dressing room. If he spoke, everyone listened. He had a stature within the side that demanded a certain standard of behaviour even without him saying anything. I have a huge amount of respect for him.

It wasn't quite the same with Cooky at the start. He was a bit younger – several years younger than KP and Swann, for example – and so didn't immediately have the natural authority that Strauss had enjoyed. He had long been close friends with Swanny and Jimmy, too, so becoming their captain must have been quite demanding. He had their complete support, but they seemed to feel they could get away with a little more under his leadership. It's probably relevant that he was the captain when things kicked off on the pitch in Bangladesh.

That's not meant to sound critical. Cooky has grown into the job really well and the manner in which he dealt with the pressure he was under at the start of 2014 – having lost the Ashes 5–0 and with the decision to drop KP – shows what an incredibly strong, resilient man he is. He's grown into a fine leader and he has the respect of everyone in the England dressing room. In a few years, people will reflect on his record as captain and batsman and wonder why anyone ever questioned him.

I must confess, I questioned him myself in his early days. I was fielding at short leg when he came out for Essex against Warwickshire in late 2003. He can only have been eighteen and it was his second first-class game. He was out for a duck in the first innings and I recall thinking, 'There's another overrated young player.' I had seen so many – literally hundreds – of them: flashy types with all the gear who can lash a couple through the covers but are nowhere to be seen when the going gets tough.

But I couldn't have been more wrong. He scored a half-century in the second innings – the first of many I was to see him make – and I had my first glimpse of the fortitude that was to make him England's greatest Test run-scorer. He is exactly the sort of player – and man – you want in your team.

I didn't know him when I came into the Test team. But he was twenty-four and already vice-captain. He was clearly the fittest guy in the team – he holds records at Loughborough for his achievements on various horrid bits of equipment – he had a great work ethic and he was very clear about the way he played and trained.

That strength of mind has been his crucial asset. While he has continued to develop his game – he added the sweep to make himself a much better player against spin bowling – he has never strayed from the basic method he had from the start: pick off anything short or on the legs; make the bowlers bowl at him. If it sounds simple, that's because it is. But it can be desperately tough to retain that simplicity amid everything that international cricket throws at you and, as I've said before, successful batting is as much about the things you don't do as those you do.

It may be his resilience that we look back on and admire most. He has endured some grim periods when his form has deserted him – probably most memorably in 2010 – and some equally grim periods where he was taking huge stick from the media, as he did during the KP debacle in 2014. But each time he comes back stronger than ever. It

has made him a more empathetic captain and, I can assure
you, he has the utmost respect of everyone in the England
dressing room.

During the summer of 2010 – even at the start of the
2010–11 Ashes series in Australia – he was really struggling. He made an ugly century against Pakistan at The
Oval – loads of his runs came through the slips and his
hundred came up when the bowler, Mohammad Asif,
threw the ball over the keeper for four overthrows. It was
an odd series, but generally their skilful bowlers had been
all over him and we departed for Australia with his confidence very low.

That tour didn't start so well for him, either. But on the
quicker pitches of Australia – and against an attack less
able to gain lateral movement – he gradually recovered
his form and confidence, resulting in a ridiculously pro-
lific series. We put together an unbroken stand of 329 in
the first Test in Brisbane, the first time we had enjoyed a
really substantial partnership, and during it we struck up
a bond that was to endure all the ups and downs there
were to follow.

He needed that Brisbane innings. He had been questioning himself for a while and I could see his confidence start
to creep back as the runs mounted. Having come through
a tough period, he was desperate to take advantage of the
situation and developed an almost insatiable appetite for
runs. We realised, during that stand, that we had a similar
mental approach to the game and some similar challenges.
I very much enjoyed batting with him. He's already broken
most England Test batting records but, however many

runs he scores, I will always be able to remind him that I got him out in the Champion County v MCC Match at Lord's in 2005, three short of scoring his second century of the match.

At the start of the next English season, the summer of 2010, I felt my place was on the line. I hadn't scored the runs I would have liked in South Africa or Bangladesh – as well as that dismissal caught off the helmet, I was adjudged run out when replays suggested I had made my ground – and I had lost my place in the T20 side.

Andy made me apologise to the team again after a T20 match against Pakistan in Dubai in February 2010. I had messed up, it's true, in making 39 from 51 balls when opening the batting. We ended up scoring 148 and Pakistan chased it down with an over to spare. But making me stand up in the changing rooms and say sorry to the rest of the lads was an unnecessary humiliation, I thought. Eoin Morgan came up to me afterwards and asked, 'What was that about? It happens.' I never played another T20 international.

It was pretty obvious in Dubai that Andy wanted to find a way to get Craig Kieswetter and Michael Lumb into the side. He asked me to move out of the way in the dressing rooms once as he was trying to watch Lumb play in the Indian Premier League on TV – which was, ironically, one of the reasons Kev was in trouble as he tried to watch his IPL side while on England duty – and I really felt like he was looking for an excuse to drop me. My innings in Dubai provided it.

To be fair, Kieswetter and opening partner Michael

Lumb proved good selections and helped England win the World T20 in the Caribbean in May. It stung not to be there, but I understood the decision.

The South Africa tour had started well – I made 28 and 69 at Centurion – but deteriorated. I know there's been some talk about my behaviour on that tour, especially towards the end, and I never felt I could explain what happened until now.

Even now, I feel I need to protect those involved a little. But if you sit down to write a book like this, you owe it to the reader who pays for it to tell the truth and provide explanations. So here's what happened.

My mum and dad had a terrible fight with my uncle before the final day of the Cape Town Test. The exact reasons aren't important but, in the heat of the moment, things were said, threats were made and the divisions became too deep to easily reconcile. I'm sorry to say, my dad and his brother haven't made up even now.

It meant that what should have been a special experience for all of us – me playing the only Test of my career on a ground that had always been important to all of us – was completely overshadowed. Going into the last day of the Test, when I was not out overnight and batting to save the game, I had hoped they would all be there to share in the experience. Instead none of them were. And instead of being free to concentrate exclusively on batting, my mind was clouded by concern for my family and anger that they would tarnish this special time with a silly fight.

My emotions were conflicted. I was furious with them, for sure. Here I was, on my first tour, and they were distracting me with a childish squabble. I thought they should have been mature enough to get along so as not to distract me. But I was also upset for them, as it seemed my cricketing career – the very thing that had united us all for so long – was going to tear us apart. I hated the idea of my dad and his brother not talking.

I blamed myself. If I had scored runs in that Cape Town Test – and I made 20 in the first innings and 42 in the second – I thought the mood would have been better and they wouldn't have argued. Runs had always made things better, you see, and I hadn't been able to score enough to make everyone happy. They had all been at The Oval and none of them argued because I scored a century.

Going into that Johannesburg Test, my mind was cluttered and distracted. There was a week off between the games and, in that time, I came to understand the severity of the argument. My dad flew back to New Zealand, where he was working, and I was so annoyed – and distracted – by my mum that I didn't want to see her.

All those old feelings came back: cricket isn't worth it if it causes this pain. And my mum's words from long ago came back, too: 'You never get runs when we've argued.'

Looking back at videos of me batting in that Test now is embarrassing. I was in no frame of mind to play. My movements are sharp and frenetic. I jump about at the crease, trying to guess where the ball is going before it is delivered, as I don't have the confidence to wait for it or the concentration to focus. In the first innings I flayed at anything anywhere near me and was soon leg before playing across a straight one. In the second innings I was on the move when I nicked one to slip.

I was in a bad enough state to confide in Andy Flower just ahead of the game. It was the first time I had let him take a peek inside my mind and allowed him to understand the thoughts that defined me and the family worries that weighed upon me. There wasn't much he could do to help, but he was supportive and as understanding as I could have reasonably expected. 'Try not to worry about it,' he said. 'We do all have these off-field pressures. We have to learn to block them out.' Which is true, but easier said than done. A few years later when he spoke on the spur of the moment, following my withdrawal from the Ashes tour, about the stress-related problems with which I had wrestled my entire career, that is what he meant.

Andy Flower:

He had a big wobble in South Africa. It was a surprise and it was a worry. He opened up about it, which was good because it allowed us to understand why it happened, but I was concerned.

He was taking on too much responsibility for his family. As if playing international cricket against a good side wasn't enough, he seemed to have taken it upon his shoulders to set the mood for his entire family. I didn't think that was healthy.

Mickey Arthur, the South Africa coach at the time, was caught on camera mocking him at one stage. He was doing that thing where people signal with their

finger around the side of their face to suggest someone is
mentally ill or something. I didn't think that was right and
I didn't like it.

I've read since that I was unsettled by the pace of the South
Africa attack. It's laughable, really. Morne Morkel and Dale
Steyn are, without doubt, fine bowlers. But there are a lot
of fine bowlers out there and the thought that I had never
faced fast bowling before is ridiculous. The way I see it, I
was in no fit state to play and they were expertly equipped
to exploit my condition.

Anyway, by the time we reached the first Test of the
English summer in 2010, I felt it was make or break for me
in Test cricket. I felt in great form, though, having made a
century in the County Championship against Lancashire
and, on the morning of the game, I remember walking out
of the nets saying to Richard Halsall, the assistant coach,
'I'm ready.' I was so confident, I wanted us to lose the toss
so I could get out there and bat all day.

On a damp morning at Lord's we were duly inserted on
a green pitch and, in tricky conditions, Andrew Strauss
and I added 181 for the second wicket. He scored 87 and
I went on to get 226. True, it wasn't the strongest attack in
world cricket, but nobody else in the side made 50 – actually Eoin Morgan, with 44, was the only other guy to reach
30 – and I felt I had won some time and some respect with
that innings.

The incident that really struck me in that game was
coming into lunch on the first day. I was 50 not out and
had helped see us through a tough session, but I had the

distinct impression that Andy Flower was gutted that I
had done so. I may be wrong, but it was hard to avoid the
conclusion that he been hoping I failed so they could bring
Ravi Bopara back into the side.

It was later in the summer I played the innings that
secured my place in the team and my value in the eyes of
my teammates. The Pakistan seam attack were top class,
just about as good as it gets, and at Lord's they reduced
us to 102 for seven in conditions offering them plenty. But
Stuart Broad, who batted beautifully, and I added 332 for
the eighth wicket and we eventually went on to win the
game by an innings. It may well have been the best of my
Test centuries.

This very good Pakistan attack included Mohammad
Amir and Mohammad Asif, who used English conditions brilliantly, Wahab Riaz, who was quick but didn't
quite have the control he was to gain a few years later in
his career, and Saeed Ajmal, who was nowhere near the
bowler he was to become by the time we played them in
the UAE in 2012 but still a fine spinner. They had won the
previous Test, at The Oval, to level the series at 1–1 with
two to play, so by the time Broady joined me in the middle
they must have fancied their chances of taking a lead in
the series.

At first I thought we should just try to reach 200. Amir
was moving the ball round corners and, when the ball
wasn't swinging in, it was angled across and aiming for
the outside edge.

Stuart batted beautifully. You could see he had been
a batsman when he was growing up: he had a decent

technique and he timed the ball really sweetly. By the time they took the second new ball, a lot of the juice had left the pitch and he enjoyed the extra hardness coming on to the bat. Everything he hit went into the gaps.

It was a magical feeling. I had scored a century for Warwickshire in a pretty much empty Lord's in 2006 and I had goosebumps then. To produce this innings in front of a full house was even better. I recall walking back through the Long Room at stumps on day two, the pair of us both unbeaten with centuries. The members formed a tunnel and were cheering and applauding. It's a great memory.

That series brought us much closer as a side. It was obvious very early on that some of that Pakistan team were spot fixing. I recall overhearing Mohammad Asif ask the umpire how close his foot was to the line at Trent Bridge; it was almost as if he was encouraging him to check and call a no-ball when he overstepped.

When the story came to light in the *News of the World* we were disgusted. There was a genuine anger within the squad and, from a personal perspective, it overshadowed the effort Stuart and I had put into winning that game at Lord's. It seemed so disrespectful to us, to the game, to the spectators. Our relationship with the Pakistan team was already poor – Umar Akmal had a bizarre habit of calling me 'the Cape coloured' every time I came to the crease – and this was the last straw.

But our anger multiplied when Ijaz Butt, the chairman of the Pakistan Cricket Board, had the gall to accuse *us* of throwing the third ODI at The Oval. 'There is loud and clear talk in the bookies' circle that some English players were paid enormous amounts of money to lose the match,' Butt said. 'No wonder there was total collapse of the English side.'

Enough was enough. We were already convinced that a few of them were cheating yet now *we* were being accused by this buffoon. And nobody at the International Cricket Council or anywhere else seemed to be doing much about it.

We decided to take matters into our own hands. Ahead of the fourth ODI at Lord's, we held a meeting at the Landmark Hotel, where we were staying, with the intention of discussing whether we should refuse to finish the series.

The meeting started at about 9.30 p.m. Straussy was among those who thought we should make a stand and refuse to play. I was with him all the way. We were seeing the game we all love twisted and corrupted before our eyes. Someone had to take a stand.

It was a brave stance from Strauss, though. There would have been a lot of pressure upon him to side with the normal ECB hierarchy. To keep quiet and allow the series to finish without making a fuss. That way, the broadcasters had their games, the sponsors had their coverage and the ECB had their money.

But he proved stronger than that. He never wavered. He stood up for his team, who had been slandered and whose efforts on the pitch were being questioned and negated by the behaviour of a few players in the opposition. When most of the talk was about money, he talked morality. He was deeply impressive that night.

Giles Clarke, the ECB chairman, said he could understand our feelings and that, if we were sure, he would back
us, but we should be aware that any decision to abandon
games would have financial repercussions for the ECB.
'We'll have no choice but to cut funding for grassroots
cricket if you do this,' was the gist of his message.

In the end – and it was almost 2 a.m. by the time we had
all had our say – we held a vote. But when it finished in a
tie, Andy seemed to take it upon himself to have a casting
vote. And he thought the series should continue.

The ECB had been worried about a series being can-
celled early for a while. In 2006, Pakistan were so offended
by being accused of ball tampering during the Oval
Test – they refused to come out after tea for a while and
the umpires concluded they had forfeited the game – that
it was feared they would abandon the tour. Had that
happened, the ECB might have had to compensate the
broadcasters, sponsors and ticket holders to the tune of
many millions of pounds. After it almost happened again
in 2010, they started to pile money into a reserve account.
It was worth more than £70 million the last time I heard.

After that late-night meeting at the Landmark, we
resumed training at Lord's the next day. The atmosphere
was horrible – full of tension, with deep animosity between
the sides – and a few of us were struggling to shrug off the
resentment we felt about having to play against Pakistan.

Wahab Riaz walked past me by the nets on the Nursery
Ground and tried to eyeball me. 'You going to accuse us
of match-fixing again?' I asked.

'Your mum knows all about match-fixing,' he said.

It was a ridiculous answer but it was all I needed. I smashed my pads across his face – they made a great sound – and grabbed him by the throat. I guess I was looking for an opportunity to lash out and he had provided it. I'm not sure how things would have played out, but Graham Gooch, the England batting coach, rushed over to separate us. 'That's not how we do things, Trotty,' he said.

As a result, I was called in to see the match referee, Jeff Crowe. Riaz said he had been accused of match-fixing. It was rubbish, but it provided a convenient way for Pakistan to sustain the victim mentality that may have convinced a few of their supporters at home that they were guilty of nothing and just suffering at the hands of a biased media.

It was a part that Waqar Younis played up to. I knew Waqar pretty well from his time at Warwickshire and considered him a friend. But he was trying to save his skin as much as any of them at the time and deflecting any blame on to me or England was as good a ploy as any. I was pretty disappointed with him over that. It didn't work: I wasn't punished by the ICC or the ECB, and three of that Pakistan team ended up in prison.

Back in the dressing room, Andy was angry with my behaviour, but Straussy stuck up for me. 'What do you expect, Andy?' he said. 'We ask the guys to give everything towards winning for the team and then they're accused of cheating: this is exactly what I warned would happen.'

That was typical Andrew Strauss. He wasn't the sort to launch into Churchillian speeches before every session. He didn't need to demonstrate that he was our captain at every opportunity. He wore his responsibility lightly and didn't feel the need to remind us. But when you needed his support, you knew it was there. He had your back. And, as a result, we all had his.

To be fair to Pakistan, they were a completely different team when we played them again in 2012. They not only played some great cricket – they deservedly beat us 3–0 – but they had completely cleaned up their act. They played hard, but they played fair and they won back our respect. Salman Butt's successor as captain Misbah-ul-Haq deserves a lot of credit for the way he transformed that team.

I'm quite happy for those convicted of match-fixing – Amir, Salman Butt and Asif – to return to the game, too. They've served their time and they were all very good cricketers. I thought Asif was in decline even during that series in 2010 – he was nowhere near the bowler he had been when he played for Leicestershire earlier in his career – but Amir was a special talent. If he can turn his life around and contribute to Pakistan cricket, then all well and good. I truly hope he takes his second chance. He has a lot to offer.

Anyway, the point of all this is to show that, by the time we reached Australia at the end of 2010, we had been through a lot together. We had been tested on the pitch and seen each other perform when the pressure was on. And we had been under pressure off the pitch and trusted one another to stick together when times were tough. We were confident of our own skills and those of our teammates, and we had been moulded into a tight unit with a very

clear, shared aim: we wanted the Ashes and we wanted
them badly.

A lot has been written about that team now and, to read
some of it, you would think that we never got on. It's not
so. At that time, the time we beat Pakistan, the time we
won the Ashes, the time we beat India to reach the top of
the world rankings, we were close. Maybe it was just that
winning makes everything seem OK. But I honestly think
it was more than that. We knew we needed one another,
we were enjoying the journey we were on and we enjoyed
each other's successes. It was a golden time.

I recall us all sitting in the dressing rooms at Sydney
with the series won. Cigar smoke and laughter filled the
air. Andy Flower stood to give a speech, but no sooner had
he said 'Gentlemen . . . ' than he was shouted into silence
with a barrage of good-natured abuse. He sat down with
a big smile knowing this wasn't the time for a talk. This
was a time for celebrating. We were happy in our own
company and what we had achieved.

I cherish those memories and those friendships. I hated
it when the atmosphere soured and former friends fell out.
I've grown to like KP very much, but I begged him to back
off when he was having a go at Cooky and Matt Prior and
I regret that it's hard to envisage a way in which the whole
team will ever be able to get together and reminisce about
old times. That's a shame. As I see it, we'll always have so
much more that unites us than divides. Maybe time will
heal. I hope so.

When I look back now, I do wish I had been able to
savour the moment more. I wish I had taken the chance

to look around, see the faces of the people cheering us on, tried to soak up the sights and sounds of a full stadium when you're batting your team to victory. My first Test, at The Oval, was the first time I had played in whites at a full ground. I wish I had taken the time to appreciate it more.

But it doesn't work like that. I know that, had I tried to take it all in, I wouldn't have been as in the moment as I needed to be. I wouldn't have been concentrating on my job. I know that I wouldn't have had the focus I needed to concentrate on scoring the next five runs that was all I thought about for the first four years of my Test career.

7

THE OVAL, 2009
Debut

I expect every player recalls the moment they were told they were about to make their Test debut. I expect for most of them, it was a joyful experience. But it just made me grumpy.

For me it came at Trent Bridge in August 2009. I'd just made a century against Nottinghamshire and, on the dressing-room balcony after the game, Ashley Giles said, 'Good news, Trotty: you're going to be batting at number five at The Oval next week.'

'What about the ODI squad?' I answered. 'Aren't I in that?'

Ash's look was a mixture of amusement and exasperation. 'Trotty, did you hear me? You're going to be making your Test debut in the deciding match of the Ashes . . . '

'But I'm not in the ODI squad?'

Amazing, isn't it, that something I had worked towards

for so long, something that was so important to me, was dismissed so flippantly? I had made one of the best pieces of news I'd ever received into a complaint.

I guess, by then, I expected to be selected. I had been in the squad for the previous game, at Leeds, but the team management decided to go with Durham pace bowler Steve Harmison instead. Now, after an innings defeat at Headingley, they had decided that Ravi Bopara was going to be dropped and I was the next in line. Andy Flower had told me I was the best batsman in the squad based on our performance in the nets at Leeds. I knew there had been media speculation about Mark Ramprakash and Marcus Trescothick, but I was the one who had been in the squad and I always felt I was going to get the call.

Besides, I knew being selected was only one step on the journey. Loads of people had been selected; few of them went on to make a success of it. And I didn't want to be one of those who played a couple of games and slid back into county cricket. I'd been there and done that.

'Anyway,' Ash said, 'we'd like you to take a look at the Australian bowling. So we've included you in the Lions team to play against them tomorrow.'

'Tomorrow?' I was aghast. There was no way I wanted that. It was Friday evening when we had that conversation and he wanted me to drive from Nottingham to Kent for a two-day game starting the next morning before joining up with the England squad on Tuesday night in London. The Test started on Thursday.

So I made one of the best decisions of my life. I asked

if I could skip the Lions match, have the weekend off and join up with the Test squad as planned on Tuesday night.

'You'll have to phone Andy Flower,' Ash said. 'It'll be up to him.'

I hardly knew Andy at the time. He was clearly a bit surprised by my call and suggested I might benefit from the exposure to the Australian attack. And, if I hadn't just made a hundred, I might have agreed with him. But I felt confident enough to stick to my guns and insist that I would benefit most of all from three days at home.

'Give me five minutes to think about it,' he said, in that very deliberate manner he has.

He soon phoned back. 'Yes, that's fine,' he said. 'I trust you to know what's best for you.'

Looking back now, I'm impressed I had the confidence to make such a request. And regretful that, at the end of the 2013 season, I didn't make a similar request. Maybe it would have made all the difference? Or maybe it would just have delayed what happened next?

Batting takes a lot out of me. The way I play, when I'm at my best anyway, requires immersion in the moment. It requires complete concentration. It requires absolute focus and discipline. If I'm tired mentally or physically, that level of concentration is hard to find. Maybe it's different for other people – though I doubt it – but the balance between fresh and in-form is delicate for me and gaining the right amount of rest was crucial. It wasn't a balance I was always able to strike.

The benefits of going into my debut fresh were obvious straight away. There was a huge amount of noise out on the pitch when I went to face my first delivery. It wasn't just the crowd – though that was a culture shock for a first-class game – but the Australian fielders. I loved it: the abrasive atmosphere just heightened my senses. This was where I wanted to be; this was where I had *always* wanted to be.

Ashley Giles:

When he came into the team at The Oval in 2009, there was no one I would rather have batting for my life. I guess you never know for certain how someone will react in that situation, but I had a huge amount of confidence in him. There was no one in the country – not Mark Ramprakash, who was another option – who could have gone into that game – a deciding Test in the Ashes, remember – with so little baggage and so much assurance. He had no doubts. He was confident and he was ready.

I had no doubts. Not for a moment did I feel out of my depth. I was right behind my first delivery – a good-length ball from Peter Siddle which I played off the front foot into the covers – and so in my zone that I was able to block out everything. I was standing at short leg getting ready to face the next ball, when Ian Bell's voice finally pierced my consciousness.

'It's the end of the over, Trotty,' he was saying. 'You're not on strike.'

After I was out in the first innings – brilliantly run out by Simon Katich, at short leg, who stopped a pretty firm flick and threw down the stumps before I could regain my ground – I sat in the dressing room with my pads still on and the sweat dripping onto the floor.

Andy stuck his head round the door. 'Well played, Trotty,' he said. 'Enjoy it?'

'It's the most fun I've ever had,' I answered instinctively. And it was. It was everything I had ever wanted and everything I had dreamed it would be. The intensity was high, the standard was high and you felt that every moment mattered. I had been confident going into the match, but I had just proved to myself that I could cut it at that level. I was very happy.

Andy Flower:

He came into the England set-up with a bad reputation. It wasn't that he was seen as difficult or anything. It was that he had a reputation for selfishness.

I just couldn't see any sign of that. He bought into everything we were trying to do. From running from fine leg to fine leg between overs or even deliveries, to the way he prepared before games and the way he spoke in meetings. He came into the team fully formed as a player, I suppose. He was confident, he knew his game and he was hungry. He was ready for international cricket and he contributed beyond what he offered with the bat.

Sometimes people mistake single-mindedness for selfishness and I think that was what had happened with Trotty. You need an extra bit of determination to carry

you through the tough times, I think. It can make all
the difference in tight encounters. He was a very good
team man. But he was also very driven and focused. I
could see that and I liked it. That single-mindedness, that
determination, it oozed out of him.

He had a beautiful method. He was really solid and
played with the full face of the bat. He knew his game
inside out.

Ahead of the Leeds Test, he batted really well in some
tricky nets. He made some difficult bowling appear
simple. He was solid and confident.

I could understand why he didn't want to play against
Australia right ahead of the Test. One view was that it gives
you a chance to look at their bowling, but it also gives
them a chance to look at your batting. I could understand
not wanting them to give them that opportunity.

But it was exhausting. The toll of batting to that level, in
that situation, for that long (I was at the crease for five and
a half hours in making my second-innings century) left me
shattered by the end of the game. Emotionally, as much as
anything, I was spent. And then, at the end of the match,
when I thought we could relax in the dressing room, I was
required to do the round of media interviews that are now
part and parcel of a player's day.

I had no idea at the time. 'What, I have to go and stand
on the outfield and be interviewed by Mike Atherton?' I
said in disbelief. I thought I was free to go after I did that
one, but then there were more TV interviews, and then
radio interviews and then the written press. It seemed to

go on for ever. Thank God I took that break, I remember thinking. It's no coincidence that, throughout my career, I tended to do better towards the start of series.

It wasn't the first time I'd asked for a break. At the end of the 2008 county season, I was included in the Hong Kong Sixes squad and was then meant to come home and spend several weeks training at Loughborough before a Performance Squad trip to India.

I was exhausted. I'd worked really hard that season and, helping Warwickshire gain promotion, had won the club's player of the year award. I'd scored well over 1000 first-class runs and averaged more than 60. I felt I'd taken a significant step forward in terms of my consistency and attitude.

But by the time I got to Loughborough, I could feel my enthusiasm for the game ebbing away. I just didn't want to play cricket. I wanted to sleep in my own bed, see my friends and family and have some down time before doing it all again. After one day of training, I approached Dave Parsons, who was academy director at the time, and told him how I felt. He understood and I was given several weeks off.

Why didn't I do something similar in 2013? Maybe because, in both 2008 and 2009, I had performed well, so I felt I was requesting the break from a position of strength. In 2013, I felt I wasn't contributing so I had to work harder – or at least be seen to work harder – and didn't feel I could justify such a request. I'm pretty certain that, if I'd explained to Andy how I felt ahead of the ODI series in 2013, he would have understood.

Alastair Cook:

I didn't know Trotty much before that game between
England and Warwickshire ahead of the 2009 Ashes,
but during it I recall thinking, 'Jeez, this guy can really
play.'

It wasn't that he scored many runs. It was that, while
everyone else looked hurried and uncomfortable, Trotty
lined the ball up well, seemed to have the time to play it
and looked as if he was enjoying the challenge. Freddie
bowled quick in that game. He was trying to prove his
fitness, so he really charged in and some of Trotty's
teammates didn't look as if they fancied it at all.

Andy Flower was clearly impressed, too. I remember
him asking me what I had thought of Trotty at the time
and it was pretty obvious to all of us that he was one to
look out for.

It probably took us a year to get to know him and
understand what a genuine guy he was. He had his
idiosyncrasies – the marking of the guard and the
fiddling with his pads – which you noticed more as you
batted with him, and he dressed unusually badly off the
pitch.

There had been a suggestion, before he played for us,
that he could be selfish and you could see how people
could come to that conclusion. He loved to bat and he
loved to score more runs than anyone else. We didn't see
that as a bad thing – why would we? – so he was allowed
to play to his strengths with England, which was to bat
and bat and score as many runs as he could.

I had actually first played for England in 2007.

No, I hardly remember it, either. It was over before it began, really. I played two T20 internationals against West Indies, making 9 in the first and 2 in the second.

It wasn't a wasted experience, though. It was a sharp wake-up call. I learned how far off the pace I was and how much improvement I'd have to make if I was going to be a success at international level.

I didn't give myself the best chance in those first two games. I was in the middle of the worst season of my career and I'd broken my left hand facing Liam Plunkett in the nets before the first match. I had an X-ray at the time which didn't show anything untoward but, when it was still causing me pain a couple of weeks later, another X-ray showed a clear break. I went out to field for the first time as an international cricketer having taken three co-codamol and, as a consequence, feeling bizarrely relaxed.

I do have a funny memory of that first time with the England squad. As I didn't really know anyone – I hadn't even been on a Lions tour – I didn't understand what they all did. I recall looking at Mark Saxby, the team masseur, who accompanied me to hospital for my X-ray, and thinking 'What the hell is your job meant to be?' A few years later, I came to understand that he was the heartbeat of the team. The man who everyone could trust. The man who many of us relied upon to pick us up when we were down and in whom we confided. He really is the unsung hero of that England team.

I owed my selection to Peter Moores. While I didn't really know him either, I had tended to score heavily against Sussex when he was their coach and I had clearly left an impression. As well as a century on Warwickshire debut in 2003 – I opened the batting and was 96 not out by lunch against an attack that included Mushtaq Ahmed, James Kirtley and Jason Lewry – I made ninety against them in 2004, a double hundred in 2005 and 109 in 2006. I guess that, even after he had moved on from the club, Moores kept a close eye on their fortunes. And, I know I no longer have any reputation as a T20 player – let's not get into that here – but despite having hardly played in the format for a few years, I am (at the time of writing) actually still Warwickshire's highest run-scorer in T20 cricket.

I was fortunate in that I developed in a period when county cricket was strong. The move to two divisions, with promotion and relegation, had been taken in 2000 with four-day County Championship cricket also becoming standard. As a consequence, every result mattered and county cricket became tougher and more competitive. Former Australian opener Justin Langer, who captained Somerset for a while, remarked that county cricket was as high a standard of domestic cricket as he had experienced.

Part of that strength came from the Kolpak players within the domestic game. Kolpak players – players who qualified to play in England through a loophole that insisted that freedom of movement applied not just to EU citizens but to those whose countries had trade agreements with the EU – typically came from southern Africa and included the likes of Murray Goodwin, Dale Benkenstein, Martin van Jaarsveld, Claude Henderson, Heath Streak and many, many more.

If you're a young bowler trying to dismiss Goodwin, you learn how tough international cricket can be. And if you're a batsman trying to take on Henderson or Streak, you will gain some idea how much control and skill international bowlers have. Together, such players helped narrow the gap between the domestic and the international game. It is, I am convinced, one of the contributory reasons that four of us in the top seven (Andrew Strauss, Alastair Cook, Matt Prior and I) of the England team that reached number one in the Test rankings were able to hit the ground running at the top level and score centuries on debut. Two others (Ian Bell and Kevin Pietersen) made half-centuries.

While there is not much disputing the complaint that the balance between 'home-grown' and 'bought-in' players went too far towards Kolpak registrations – there was an infamous game between Northants and Leicestershire where more than half the players involved were not eligible to play for England – there was something to be said for the improvement in standard that a controlled number of Kolpak (and similar) registrations brought to the game.

Since then, the ECB have incentivised clubs to field young, England-qualified players. The optimum payments are made if two of the players are aged under twenty-two and three more are under twenty-six on 1 April of the year concerned. It is a move that, at the smaller clubs in particular, has squeezed some experienced players out of the game prematurely and allowed young players into the game a bit too quickly. At times now, especially towards the bottom of Division Two, you have teams of kids playing one another. Of course it is important to provide opportunity, but we don't want to make it too easy, either.

Meanwhile, the ECB have also made it harder for any sort of player not qualified for England – including overseas players – to gain work permits. If these criteria had been in force at an earlier time, Graeme Hick and Viv Richards would have been unable to play county cricket at the early stage of their careers.

This has, in my view, diluted the standard of county cricket and made the gap between the domestic and international games much wider.

I also benefited from the 2005–6 winter playing for Otago in New Zealand. But it wasn't just about playing. I learned a bit more about taking responsibility. I wasn't very old – only twenty-four – but, as the overseas player and a veteran of all of two T20 international caps for England, I was seen as a senior player and expected to behave as such.

That was a bit of a culture shock. At that stage, I had always been the promising young player pushing for greater recognition. It sort of came with the territory to be a bit of a tearaway.

Early on there was an incident where I was frustrated with my batting in a net session. I was so furious that, when I reached the dressing room, I smashed the bin with my bat. Then, consumed with shame, I tried to hide my crime. I took a bus into town, bought an identical bin and snuck it back into the pavilion before anyone realised. The only mistake I made was putting the old, broken bin in the new one. It didn't take too long for someone to work out what had happened. The guys all had a good laugh about that. And I realised I had to grow up a bit.

One of the things that struck me from that trip was the effort Mike Hesson made upon my arrival. As coach, he was arguably the most important man at the club, but he made the journey out to Dunedin airport to pick me up himself and made sure I was settled in and felt welcomed.

Mike has a rare humility as a coach. He knew that he hadn't played the game to the level of the players in the teams he coached – he was Otago's B team keeper, but never graduated to the first team – and he never tried to compensate for that. He didn't try and force his views on anyone and he would sometimes say 'you guys might understand this more than me' or similar.

I was put in a house on a hill above the city with four other players. Rumour had it the house was haunted and pretty soon a rumour went round that it was cursed.

It's true that we all suffered from injury. Neil Broom managed two balls in the entire season before tearing his intercostal muscles. Aaron Redmond managed to dislocate his knee taking a catch on the boundary and James McMillan, a fast bowler who slept on a blow-up mattress on the floor (I would be woken at about 3 a.m. each night by the sound of him having to inflate it again), funnily enough suffered with a bad back. And Greg Todd suffered the worst injury I've seen in person on a pitch when he caught his studs in the turf while trying to take the ball and saw his foot remain in place while his body twisted the other way. The end result was that one of his feet was left facing 180 degrees in the wrong direction. It was so bad that I had to run off the pitch, push Chris Cairns out of the toilet, and vomit several times. It was like a cricket-themed version of *The Exorcist*, though I don't expect my head actually spun round. Later we visited him in hospital, where his operation was delayed by a major car accident.

I ended up with a stress fracture in my back, too, from all the overs I bowled. But I had a great season on and off the pitch and was named New Zealand's domestic player of the year at the end of it.

Those Kiwis sure are tough. At the start of the trip I recall playing a game of touch rugby as a warm-up. The ball was passed my way and, the next thing I knew, I was lying on the floor having received a heavy tackle.

'Ahh, yeah, Trotty,' one of my colleagues said. 'Touch rugby doesn't mean quite the same thing here ... '

Damn right. The county is obsessed with rugby and its influence has seeped into their cricket. The team are as easy-going as any off the field, but they have become hard as hell on it. I remember David Saker telling me to hold the bat in my left hand at the non-striker's end and encouraging me to block off the bowler if he needed to run into the leg side to field the ball. But I tried it when Nathan McCullum was bowling one time and he just dived straight through me. He literally reacted as if I wasn't there and made for the ball with no thought for his safety – or mine. They breed them tough out there.

That 2007 season – the season I made my international debut – was a bit of a disaster for me. It was the first season I was eligible to play for England and I put myself under too much pressure to perform. Having scored 1000 first-class runs for three seasons in succession, I didn't manage 500 that year. Near the end of it, I recall Keith Cook, the cricket operations manager at Warwickshire, coming into the changing rooms and mentioning that they had drafted a contract extension should I be interested in looking at it. I took it off him and signed it without even looking at the figures. I was just desperate to stay and grateful for anything.

I wasn't helped by the environment at Warwickshire. The coach, Mark Greatbatch, a former New Zealand player, seemed like a nice enough guy at first but, as things deteriorated on the pitch, his relationship with many in the team deteriorated with it. He fell out spectacularly badly with one of most respected and long-serving players, Dougie Brown. Things weren't helped when Greatbatch brought in psychologist Dave Hadfield who quickly realised that he was a major part of the problem. We were relegated in both competitions – the County Championship and the List A league – at the end of the season.

I had felt alienated from our pre-season tour to Grenada. We had, as ever, a meeting in which they made some laboured point about us all striving to achieve 'True North' – which, as far as I could tell among the psychobabble and bullshit, was meant to represent the ultimate contribution to the team. We were then asked to mark on a board the position we thought we warranted at present.

Well, I had been the only man at the club to make 1000 first-class runs the previous season. And I'd done it the two seasons before that, too. So I felt fairly well justified in marking myself somewhere in the north-east region.

Even more so, after pretty much everyone else marked themselves in the same area.

But then Greatbatch turned the chart over and showed where the coaches thought we merited being placed. I was pretty much south. I remember looking at the chart in disbelief and thinking, 'How the hell have you worked that out?' I became even more annoyed as I realised I was just about the only player to be marked so low. Being top run-scorer must count as some sort of positive contribution, I thought.

The one good thing that did come out of that tour was that I roomed with Ashley Giles. Odd though it may sound, I hadn't really got to know him before that. He was busy with England and, when he did play for us, it was always with a view to gaining fitness or form. At that time, he had his head down trying to win his place back in the England side and a lot on his mind. He had returned home early from the Ashes after his wife, Stine, had been diagnosed with a brain tumour. He was to become a major figure in my development.

Abi:

When he got off the coach at Edgbaston following that pre-season tour, he looked grey and ill. He was so upset by Mark Greatbatch. I think we could all see what they were trying to do – and yes, no doubt there were times Jonathan could be a bit of a brat – but they weren't encouraging or motivating. They just destroyed him. They made him feel uncomfortable in the dressing room and judged out on the pitch. He had an awful season in 2007 and it was all because they made him feel worthless and selfish and unwanted.

The good thing that came of that pre-season tour was his relationship with Ashley Giles. Very early on, Ash told him, 'If you carry on like this, you'll never play for England.' But his advice was much more specific than that. He got him writing his aims in a little book ahead of each game. He would think about exactly what he was trying to achieve and jot just a few words down to help him focus on that and allow him to judge himself after the match had finished.

He used to have ferocious rows with Ash. I was alerted to him arriving home one day when I heard shouting outside. I peered out of the window and he was bellowing at someone down the phone in the car. Then I heard Ash's voice shouting right back at him. But Ash knew which buttons to press and when. He knew when to back off and when to drive him on. The crucial thing was, Jonathan knew Ash wanted what was best for him so he accepted every challenge he was given.

But not until the end of the season. Not until I had laboured for several months, putting myself under pressure to score heavily and force my way into the Test team.

I think, in those days, I was over-reliant on my talent to take me to success. I knew I had pretty good hand–eye co-ordination and a history of making runs at every level I had played. It's not that I was afraid of hard work, either, I would go to the nets for hours. I always put in the hours.

But I can see now that I wasn't training in an especially smart or calculated way.

Certainly in that 2007 season, I wasn't doing myself any favours. Looking too far ahead and putting myself under pressure, I ended up asking Abi to feed the bowling machine for me at Edgbaston so I could have a net at about 7.30 in the morning. There didn't seem to be anyone else I could ask.

It was kind of her to agree to do it – especially given the mood I was in for much of the time – but it's probably fair to say she doesn't have a future in cricket coaching. She was afraid to put her hands too close to the machine, fearing that her fingers would be caught by the moving parts. So she was sort of dropping, or even lobbing, the balls in from what she thought was a safe distance. Sometimes she missed the machine entirely; at other times the balls would spit out unexpectedly and with bizarre amounts of spin upon them. It wasn't the best hour or two of our lives together.

So it was a huge blessing for me when Ash was appointed Warwickshire coach at the end of the season. Poor Greatbatch, whose heart was probably in the right place but really struggled, was sacked the moment the season finished and, the day after, Ash was given the job. The day after that, he called me in for a meeting.

'We need to sort you out,' he said. 'You could be, behind Ian Bell, the best batsman at this club. And you could be pushing for the Test team. You could be a top, top player. But you have to improve the way you do everything.'

It might, at another time of my career, have seemed

confrontational. But at that moment it was the guidance I had been crying out for from a coach. I felt encouraged that he rated me so highly and thought I was worth extra investment.

Over the next few weeks, Ash gave me a checklist against which I was to train every day. The headings were batting, bowling, fielding and lifestyle. Nothing too revolutionary there. But each section was broken down into sub-categories so that I was given specific things to work on. For example, the fielding section had sections on 'hitting the stumps' with my throws – I was to aim for a 95 per cent success rate – while the batting section urged me to work on new strokes. It meant that, rather than just going into the nets and hitting balls for an hour every day, I went to training with a sense of exactly what I was trying to achieve.

By the time the next season started, he had switched my focus from, as he would put it, outcomes to processes. That is, I'd learned not to focus on scoring runs as much as batting as well as I could. So I didn't look too far ahead, I didn't aim for targets and I didn't think about England. I concentrated on the next delivery, safe in the knowledge that, if I kept doing that, everything else would take care of itself.

Ashley Giles:

I thought he was a bit of a brat. He was bloody good and he knew it. He was pretty keen that we should all know it, too. It came across as brash and rude and arrogant.

I didn't know him that well until that Grenada pre-season tour. I had been away with England quite a lot as he had been breaking into the Warwickshire side and international cricket had generally been my focus.

He frustrated me. I was at the stage of my career where I knew how hard you had to work to get to the top. I wasn't the most talented cricketer in the world, but by working hard I played to a high level and enjoyed some decent success.

He was much more talented, but he was unprofessional. For me, he was typical of the Warwickshire attitude at that time: they were still dining out on the success of the team of the mid-nineties and strutting around like they had achieved something. I thought they had forgotten what it meant to represent Warwickshire and they needed shaking up.

Greatbatch and team psychologist Dave Hadfield came at him pretty hard on that tour. They wanted him to know that his behaviour wasn't acceptable. I could see what they were getting at but I think they did it in a really clumsy way. The 'True North' exercise left him feeling, 'They all think I'm rubbish and they hate me,' when it should have left him feeling 'I'm really good but I could be great and they value me enough to want to help me get there.'

That might have been my first insight into the real Trotty. He was really hurt. Not just angry, but hurt. And all that bravado, all that confidence, disappeared. We talked for hours. I tried to explain that they had the right reasons for wanting him to change and that it was for his own good. I saw a sensitive, confused side to him and realised that the brattish exterior was all a bit of an act. He is a very soft-hearted guy.

Once I saw that, I felt I knew how to make a connection with him. The relationship became quite parental, I suppose, though I generally took quite a hard line with him. I'm a pretty strict dad, too, so I'd describe it as 'tough love'. I was cruel to be kind. At times I would confront him on things to the point where he would break down and cry, but I hope I also made it clear that I was there to listen and be supportive. My own feelings were it was working very well.

The contrast between the public image and the reality with Trotty was probably greater than in anyone else I've known. I've not seen such extremes. He is a complex guy, who can seem hard and arrogant, but actually needs an arm round the shoulder and a lot of reassurance. I think everyone needs reminding how good they are, really, but he needed it more than most, while at the same time sometimes giving the impression that he was the most confident guy in the world.

I could see similarities with KP there. I think they understood one another in that way. They had that facade of extreme self-confidence, but it was wafer-thin.

Ashley reconnected Warwickshire with its past. The club had enjoyed unprecedented success in the mid-1990s, winning six trophies in little over twenty-four months at one stage, including a treble in 1994. A few guys who had been at the club in those days remained when I arrived and they passed on some of the spirit and wisdom of those teams.

One of those was Dominic Ostler. He'd emerged as a key batsman during those mid-nineties years and he used to tell a story about the man-management skills of Dermot Reeve, Warwickshire's inspirational captain. One day, Dominic – a pretty sensitive guy who worried far more about his game than you would have guessed when you saw him bludgeoning the ball to all parts on the pitch – was sitting in the players' dining room, fretting about his future at the club, when Dermot entered the room.

'What's the matter?' Dermot said.

'I haven't been in great form,' Dom said. 'I'm worried I might lose my place.'

'Mate,' Dermot replied. 'You're our best player. You're the first name on the team sheet for every game and you will be for every game in the season. If you want to go and work on something in the nets, let's do it, but you don't have to worry about your place.'

It's what every player wants to hear. You want the security and the confidence. Dermot, who really does have one of the best cricket brains I've ever come across, had the ability to make you feel ten feet tall and utterly indestructible and he passed on some of those skills to Ashley. As long as you worked hard and played for the team, those guys would back you all the way.

Greatbatch wasn't like that. He came across as negative and sour. Maybe he would have made a decent coach of another team, but he was the wrong man for Warwickshire.

Ashley replacing him was like throwing open the curtains on a dark room on a beautiful summer's day.

It was on Ashley's advice that I gave up alcohol. Well, I might have a drink a couple of times a year, but I decided that if I was really serious about being as fit as I could be, it was something else I should cut out. It was just what I thought of as a one per-center: the sort of small lifestyle change that might, in conjunction with an improved diet, extra gym sessions, enough sleep and the use of hypno-therapy – which I also started at around that time – result in an improved performance. I read a few years later that I had given it up as I had an alcohol problem. It was complete rubbish.

I guess I can understand how that rumour spread. While other guys will routinely have a beer at the close of play – it's usually to celebrate someone doing well – I would only ever have a coke or a juice. But if we won a series, we would go out and I would let my hair down to the extent that I would drink loads. As a result, I was probably the worse for wear in front of the team a fair few times.

Maybe, at university, I drank too much. My parents hardly drank – my father never did – so I never saw alcohol at home. When I arrived at university, like many students I suppose, I over-indulged in my new-found freedom. But it didn't take long for me to realise that if I was serious about my cricket – and I always was – alcohol was incompatible. It's not that I was turning up with a hangover or anything like that, but I always needed to concentrate hard to bat successfully and alcohol – even a few days before a game – impaired that just a little.

Anyway, I went on holiday at the end of the 2007 season with pretty much no idea what I was going to do that winter. Given my poor form and my poor performance for England in the T20s, I wasn't expecting to be called upon by the ECB.

But, just as I landed in San Francisco – I wanted to watch the 49ers – I received a text on my phone from the England Academy manager, Guy Jackson, telling me I'd been selected for the Performance Programme tour that winter. I was so surprised that I replied asking whether he had the wrong number.

Fortunately, it was no mistake. Just when Ash's belief and advice had revived me, I was given the opportunity to travel to India before Christmas to put into place everything he had been saying. I made a century in my first innings, 82 in my second and was then included in the Lions squad to return to India at the end of January. It felt like a second chance.

Walking off at the close of day two of the Melbourne Test in December 2010. I had an unbeaten century and we knew the Ashes were ours. Judging by all the empty seats, so did the Australian supporters. *(Tom Shaw/Getty Images)*

We retained the Ashes in Melbourne and celebrated with the families in the dressing room. Those are the special moments you cherish after you've retired. I was man of the match in that game and it was lovely to share the celebrations with Abi and Lily.

This was special. In Sydney after we'd won the Ashes in January 2011. I always enjoyed celebrating with my mum and dad. I loved to make them proud and show my gratitude for the support and encouragement that helped me become an international cricketer.

Winning the England Cricketer of the Year award at Lord's in May 2011 was a reminder of how quickly things could change. A year earlier on the same ground I felt I was about to be dropped. *(Matthew Lewis/Getty Images)*

May 2011: we must have been in trouble here as Ian Bell is asking me to bowl. He was captaining Warwickshire while Jim Troughton was injured. Belly and I have grown up together as cricketers and I have a huge amount of respect for him. *(Philip Brown)*

Winning the ICC Player of the Year as my good friend Cooky won Test Player of the Year seemed to underline the progress we were making as a team. It was great to share such times with guys who understood how tough it was to succeed at that level and who you admired on and off the pitch.

(Tom Dulat/Getty Images)

Lily playing with my ICC Player of the Year award the day after the ceremony.

I always enjoyed batting with Alastair Cook. We batted together 51 times in Test cricket – more often than I batted with any other player – and added 2711 runs at an average of 55.32. We put on 10 century partnerships. He was wonderfully calm and reassuring. *(Philip Brown)*

I enjoyed batting with KP, too. He absorbed so much pressure, the opposition were so worried about him murdering the bowling. This picture was taken as I reached fifty at Edgbaston in 2010. No Warwickshire player has ever made a Test century on the ground; a record I was unable to change. *(Philip Brown)*

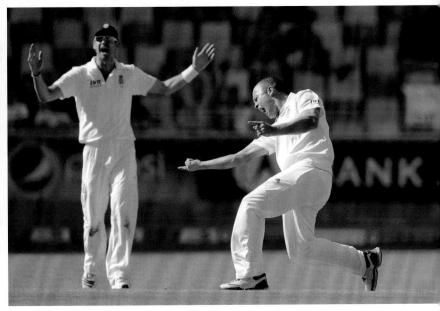

No wonder I'm pleased: I had just trapped Younis Khan leg before with one that nipped back. I considered myself a proper all-rounder until I was about seventeen, when I realised I couldn't bowl any quicker. *(Philip Brown)*

At the end of the series in the UAE, 2012. We had lost 3-0 and it seemed that everything we had worked so hard for was crumbling beneath us. *(Philip Brown)*

Making a century in Galle, 2012. It was England's first Test century against spin that winter, after we had been hammered in the UAE. It gave me a lot of confidence to make runs on a pitch that turned loads and in the hottest conditions in which I played. *(Philip Brown)*

Too good. I was batting well at Lord's in 2012 and felt I could take England to victory. Then Dale Steyn got one to rear on a good pitch and it flew in-between first and second slip. Nobody else would have caught it – look how Graeme Smith has hardly moved – but Jacques Kallis was unbelievable in the slips and held on. I always enjoyed playing against South Africa. They played hard and fair. Dale rushed down the pitch afterwards showing seven fingers to remind everyone that he had dismissed me seven times in Test cricket. Not in a mocking way; just as a celebration.

(Philip Brown)

Having a drink in Leopold's in Mumbai with Mark Saxby in November 2012. Sax has been a true friend to me. I'm hugely grateful for his support. He is the unsung hero of the England team.

Lord's may be the home of cricket, but the Wankhede Stadium in Mumbai seems like its spiritual home to me. It was a thrill to play there. Even if I was out for a duck in my only Test on the ground. *(Philip Brown)*

This picture makes me smile. I had just hit one from Ravi Jadeja for four and the India fielders were furious. The ball slipped out of Jadeja's hand as he delivered it and dribbled along the pitch. Often, in those situations, the batsman lets the ball go and the umpire calls 'dead ball'. But I smacked it through mid-wicket. In this picture Virat Kohli is letting me know what he thinks of me and I'm giving as good back to him. Virat and I get on fine, though. I knew he was going to be one of the very best the first time I saw him. After I hit that four, I could hear KP – all the way back in the dressing room – laughing. *(BCCI)*

The moment it all went wrong? My dismissal in the final of the 2013 ICC Champions Trophy at Edgbaston, stumped off a leg-side wide. The ball turned miles; probably more than any other I faced in my career. It still hurts that I didn't win that game for the side. It was, I think, a life-changing moment for a few of us. *(Michael Steele/Getty Images)*

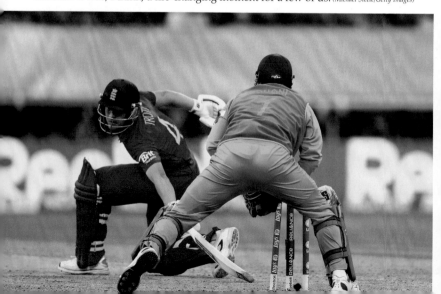

8

LEEDS, 2013
Trott's Fault

Abi:

Somehow the outside world grew much louder in the summer of 2013. Those interviews after the Leeds Test really shocked him. He just couldn't believe the media didn't understand and it made him realise how great the divide was between those in the dressing room and those outside.

He had, in the past, been so disciplined about not checking the media and not reading Twitter. But as his confidence declined, he started to look more often. He had always been aware that a few people said he batted too slowly or that he was boring, but he had no idea of the ferocity of the abuse that was out there. It hurt and shocked him.

He thought he was doing a job for the team and he took great pride in that. To see people accuse him of selfishness struck him to the core.

It was always particularly hurtful when former professionals had a go at him. He thought they should understand how tough it was. But you see some of those guys falling over themselves to be critical because it's the only way they can get a gig as a pundit. Jonathan will never do that, I promise you.

In some ways, I think it was always harder for people to warm to him because of the South African background. It made people suspicious and resentful.

I recall the exact moment I started to let the media bother me.

It was May 2013 and we had just beaten New Zealand in a Test at Leeds by 247 runs. I thought that was a pretty good effort. Yet when I gave an interview to BBC radio that night, all the questions were negative. You would have thought we had been thrashed.

Instead of being asked about Alastair Cook's century or Graeme Swann's ten wickets in the match, I was asked why England didn't enforce the follow-on and why I didn't score more quickly on the third evening. It quickly became apparent that the radio interview was representative of the views of a fair proportion of the media. They were unimpressed with our victory. They thought we should have done better.

I was shocked. How could they not understand? How could they disrespect the game, or New Zealand, so much? How could they not see that, with a four-man attack, we rarely thought about enforcing the follow-on? How could they not remember that, in the three-match series that preceded this, in New Zealand, we had been fortunate to escape with a 0–0 draw, with Matt Prior and Monty Panesar helping bat out time in one game? How could they not understand that we didn't want to have a situation where we batted last on a deteriorating pitch?

Do you know why I didn't score more quickly that evening? Because it was bloody hard. New Zealand had two very good seamers in Tim Southee and Trent Boult, and Kane Williamson was bowling outside off stump into Boult's foot holes. We were determined not to let them back into the match and I felt I had to get through it. I was under no instructions; I just went out there to bat. I finished with 76 from 164 balls and was out the next morning chasing a wide one as I tried to set up a declaration.

It is true there was some bad weather around. The whole first day of the game was washed out and we only squeezed in about forty-five minutes' play before lunch on that final day. And it's true that, at the end, Andy said I could have looked to bat a little more urgently on the third evening.

But we beat a good side by nearly 250 in just over three days' playing time. We won the series 2–0. To this day, I believe that some of the media were angry we didn't win more quickly as they had made plans to go and play golf on that final day. It was just a reminder of how far we had come and how much people now expected of us. Later that summer, we won the Ashes 3–0 and the media again treated our victory with a shrug that seemed to say, 'Is that all?' They had lost sight of how hard it is to win a

Test. We had become, to some extent, the victims of our own success. Winning didn't seem to be celebrated now; it was to be expected.

Andy Flower:

The reputation of that England team irritates me. All too often, I see it described as attritional, but we had players of huge skill and flair. Is Kevin Pietersen an attritional player? Was Matt Prior or James Anderson or Graeme Swann or Ian Bell? It's not an accurate description as far as I'm concerned. We had some very exciting players and that description is, at best, a simplification.

I'm not surprised Trotty was frustrated by our coverage at that stage. I think everyone involved was frustrated by the coverage of the 2013 Ashes. We won 3–0 and yet we were still criticised. There's no way we were given the credit we deserved for that series. But the Australian coach, Darren Lehmann, is a personable guy and he had some of the media eating out of the palm of his hand.

By that stage, we had won four of the last five Ashes series and I think the sense of how special that was had worn off a little bit. It's damn tough to win the Ashes.

The incident wasn't, in itself, a big deal. But it started me thinking. It started me wondering how people watching could perceive what we were doing so differently, started me thinking how everything thing I did was being interpreted negatively by someone, somewhere. Ridiculous though it sounds, I started thinking I needed to prove people wrong rather than just sticking to what I did best: concentrating on the moment; watching the ball; batting.

Until that moment, I was hardly aware that I had been criticised for the way I played ODI cricket. Until that moment, I had hardly bothered to think about how people might perceive what I was doing. Until that moment, I had no idea there was a hashtag on Twitter labelled #Trottsfault.

The Trottsfault thing was actually quite funny. It started, I understand now, more as a reaction to some people blaming me for everything that went wrong than any serious attempt to criticise me. So if there was an earthquake in Panama or a postal workers' strike in Canada, somebody, somewhere would always write #Trottsfault on Twitter. They were lampooning the people who blamed me for every loss.

But behind it was the reality that some people, including certain ex-players who should have known better, were suggesting that my style of play was holding the team back and putting pressure on my teammates.

I had heard accusations of selfishness before. When Ashley Giles took over as Warwickshire coach at the start of 2008, he tore into me after I misjudged an innings against Northants at Wantage Road.

Ashley Giles:

His biggest strength – and maybe one of his biggest
weaknesses – is an inability to manage the percentages of

batting. He hates getting out. And while that is, generally, a very good quality in a batsman, it means that alarm bells ring in him when he considers any option where getting out is a possibility. He can play every shot in the book, but he likes zero-percentage batting so he denies himself the opportunity of playing many of those strokes.

He understood, though, that he needed to push on at times. So we explained to him that it was OK if he took 75 balls to get to 50 so long as he then went on to reach 100 from 100 balls. He really embraced that. He was one of those who found analysis useful so, if we said we needed to be on a certain score after thirty overs and a certain score after forty, he took that on board and, more often than not, made sure it happened.

If we were chasing 200, he was just about the best in the world. The problem came when we were chasing 300. But I was very happy with the role he played for us. He did what he was asked to do and he did it brilliantly.

Some of the criticism he received was just silly. It is so easy to look at one bloke and blame him for all the faults, but there are many pieces to the jigsaw that makes up a team and you always have to look at the thing as a whole.

I didn't think the way we played was out of date until we got back from Australia at the start of 2014. By then, a score of 300 had become what a score of 260 used to be and we had to change. We couldn't expect to win ODIs with a total of 270 any more. And whether he could have done that, I don't know. Probably not, if I'm honest.

But, at the time, we needed the foundation he

provided. There was no pressure on him to change. Sure,
there were things you wanted to tweak and improve, but
it was never a case of wanting to radically change him.
He was brilliant at what he did and, if he got it wrong
sometimes, you had to accept that as you do with any
player. We should have won the Champions Trophy,
remember. Twenty to win from sixteen balls . . . I'll never
forget that equation.

He was right, too. I didn't like to hear it at the time, but if
you bat through, finish 60 not out and your side loses with
an over to go, you've screwed up, haven't you? Especially
as, on that occasion, we had been given a pretty good platform before I came in.

The thing Ash didn't understand at that stage was just
how bad we had been before he joined us. Under Mark
Greatbatch we had been relegated in both the List A and
first-class competition the previous season and confidence
was low. I felt, rightly or wrongly, that if I failed, the team
could be skittled. I felt that, unless I batted through, we
would be bowled out.

Andrew Strauss:

There was a lot of support from within the dressing room
for the way he played in ODI cricket. We accepted that
his strength was to play the anchor role and we felt that,
in the entire world, there was hardly anyone better than
him at that role. His job was to bat us up to 40 overs.

Yes, there were times we asked him to be more

aggressive. And yes, very occasionally, there were times when we limited ourselves by progressing too slowly in those middle overs.

But we learned very quickly that you can't ask Trotty to be anyone but Trotty. A couple of times he tried to play more aggressively and it didn't look natural at all. He looked ugly and awkward and he didn't score any more quickly, anyway.

He did attract some criticism from outside the dressing room, but, within it, we appreciated the role he played and knew there was pretty much nobody better at it.

There were times we played very well. We won five or six series in succession at one stage. But we can't have too many complaints about our modest reputation. You are judged by your performances in global competitions and we played some very odd, very inconsistent cricket in the 2011 World Cup. We were hammered a few times, too, which was a reminder that we weren't as good as we would like to be, though we probably should have won the 2013 Champions Trophy.

During Trotty's period in the team, the game evolved and we probably didn't keep up with its progression. It would be hard to justify that role now but he fulfilled it very successfully.

It felt like that with England, too. Just before the 2013 ICC Champions Trophy, I was given a list of statistics concerning England's recent ODI results. I had played in seventeen of the twenty-three ODIs England had contested since the start of 2012. And of those seventeen, we had lost only two and never been bowled out for under 200. But in the six games I sat out, England were beaten four times and bowled out for under 200 on three occasions.

So yes, I felt I knew my job pretty well and I was pretty confident in how I went about it.

To this day, I refute the idea that I was being selfish. It was quite the opposite: I was trying to take responsibility. I was trying to make sure I didn't leave the job to anyone else. And not once did a captain or coach complain about the job I did in the ODI side. We often spoke about how to improve and evolve as a player – you always have to do that – and part of that improvement was finding a way to push the score on more quickly. But I felt completely supported and appreciated by them.

I earned my spot in the ODI side on the South Africa tour at the end of 2009. I opened the batting with Andrew Strauss in that series and scored 87, 9 and 52 not out in the three games I played. We won both games in which I made a half-century and we won the series, too.

By the time we played our next ODI, back home, England had won the World T20 and Craig Kieswetter had earned himself a run in the ODI side. I slipped down to number three and, after a century against Bangladesh and 69 and 53 in the first two ODIs against Pakistan, I stayed there.

There were times I got it wrong. In a World Cup match against Bangladesh in Chittagong, I thought we had done really well to score 225 on a tricky pitch. I scored 67 from 99 balls. But they chased it down with an over to spare. Then, in the quarter-final, I made 86 as we set Sri Lanka a target of 230. They reached it with more than ten overs to spare without losing a wicket.

That's probably the innings I regret the most. There were some mitigating factors – a fairly heavy dew settled on the pitch after our innings and the ball skidded on more, making life much harder for our spinners and much easier for the batsmen – but I should have pushed on. I should have made it tougher for Sri Lanka. I got that one wrong and I'm still sorry about it.

Andy Flower:

Part of our model in ODI cricket was to pick players in the top four who would bat properly. So no pinch hitters or anything like that.

Trotty was one of those top four players and he did exactly the job we asked of him. The statistics showed that, when he scored forty or more, we won most of the time. He did a really good job for us and there was a lot of support for him in the dressing room. He played to the team game plan.

The criticism of his approach was very frustrating. And unfair. I actually think the whole side was a bit better than people have generally said. We beat Australia 4–0 in the series in 2012 without Kevin Pietersen. We had a method that worked very well.

The rule changes in ODI cricket have changed the format massively. And yes, if Trotty were starting his international career now, he would have to adapt his approach to survive. But playing in the time he did, he

was a very valuable performer in a team that went top
of the world rankings and should probably have won the
Champions Trophy.

On other occasions, the criticism was ridiculous. I reckon
that if I was out cheaply and we lost – and if I was out
cheaply, we usually did lose – I would receive less criticism
than if I scored fifty and we won. I made 69 in an ODI
against Ireland on a poor wicket in Dublin. You could look
at the strike rate – 65.71 runs per 100 balls – and say it was
a terrible innings. You could say our total – 201 in 42 overs
in a rain-reduced match – was hopeless. And trust me, a
fair few in the media did.

But they were failing to understand the context. That
game was played on a poor wicket. In the circumstances,
my modestly paced innings and our apparently low total
were match-winning efforts. Eoin Morgan, our captain in
that game, made a point of saying 'Fantastic job, Trotty'
after we won. But if you looked at the scorecard without
understanding any more, you might leap to the conclusion
that we were just playing old-fashioned cricket.

My highest ODI score – 137 made against an Australian
attack that included Brett Lee, Mitchell Johnson and Shaun
Tait – helped us to a total of 333 that should have been
enough to win us the game. But then we bowled poorly –
it didn't happen often, but it could happen – and they got
home with four balls to spare.

The same thing happened against Holland in our disappointing World Cup campaign of 2011. Ryan ten Doeschate
batted really well to make a century, but we bowled far

below the standards we set ourselves and they scored nearly 300. We won the game, but it was clear that our best bowler, Jimmy Anderson, was tired after his exertions in the Ashes and, as a result, we asked a bit much of the batsmen. In that World Cup defeat against Bangladesh, we conceded thirty-three wides. That's not the batsmen's fault, is it?

A bit of a split emerged between the batting and bowling units at one stage. The bowlers – Stuart Broad, Jimmy Anderson and Graeme Swann – were generally the more dominant characters, so in team meetings they held sway over batsmen like me, Belly, Andrew Strauss and, at times, Alastair Cook. They liked to come to the batting meetings – and, to be fair, everyone bats – but they wouldn't let us come to the bowling meetings. I used to ask 'Why don't you bowl more yorkers?' and they would say 'Because they get thumped back over our heads.' They basically just shouted us down and said it was our fault when things went wrong.

It didn't matter if we scored 280 on a 250 track; if we lost, it seemed the batsmen were always to blame. However many we scored, some people thought we should have scored more. And it seemed that whoever we beat – and we made it to number one in the world ODI rankings in 2012, remember – people would say that, on better pitches, against better opposition, we would be found out. It's part of the reason that losing in the final of the 2013 Champions Trophy was such a disappointment. We had such a lot to prove; we had so many people to prove wrong.

Alastair Cook:

There is no doubt in my mind that, by the time we played the Champions Trophy final in 2013, we were – in our own conditions – the best ODI side in the world. We probably should have won that final, but it became a twenty-over game on a pitch that was, for whatever reasons, turning square against the T20 world champions. It wasn't what we had been expecting but we still should have won.

Trotty was a highly valued member of that side and played a huge role in taking us to number one in the world rankings. The game has probably changed quite a lot from the time when he and I were in that team but, at the time, he won us a lot of games. The analysts worked out that we scored, on average, about twenty-five more runs each time he played and we became the sort of side who were hard to beat.

Yes, if someone came in and played a fantastic innings against us, as Kumar Sangakkara did at The Oval in the group stages of that tournament, we could be beaten. But it felt as if that sort of performance was required to deny us.

Sometimes people talked as if the role I played in ODIs was easy. Well, look how many other people have managed it. Despite a disappointing end to my ODI career, I finished with a batting average of 51.25; that's almost ten higher than the next highest average (Joe Root, with 41.90 at the time of writing) of any England player to have featured in fifty or more ODIs. In the entire history of

ODIs, only A.B. de Villiers, Virat Kohli, Michael Bevan and Hashim Amla of regular, full nation players average more than me. My strike rate (77.07 runs per 100 balls) wasn't the quickest, it is true, but it compares OK to Kumar Sangakkara (78.86) and Mahela Jayawardene (78.96), and I don't recall them suffering from #sangasfault hashtags.

When England thrashed their three highest ODI scores within a couple of weeks in June 2015, I watched with as much admiration as anyone. And I'd accept it showed how far the game had come: the rule changes; the influence of T20 cricket; the all-out aggression. I could see that the game had moved on and there was no place for my style of play any more.

But I'm not sure it will always be that way. We may well come to look back on 2015 as a freak year. Already the ICC have acted to protect bowlers a little more with new regulations concerning the fielding restrictions and, by the time the next ICC Champions Trophy or World Cup come round, I can see sides returning to a more conventional approach.

Both those tournaments are scheduled to be played in relatively early-season England with two new balls. Sides are going to need someone to play the anchor role at times, or we're going to see them bowled out in thirty-five overs.

One of the criticisms of the England side that I played in is that we were driven by stats. And it's true, Nathan Leamon, the analyst, did have a strong influence during those years. He would, for example, tell us what an average score was on a certain surface, what a winning score was likely to be and provide a benchmark for the score we should be looking to have made at twenty, thirty and forty overs.

Graeme Swann was one of those who never liked it. He always felt the batsmen should just smash it as much as they could and, to be fair to him, he always played like that. You can't always smash good bowlers, though. You've still got to have the skill to see off good spells or judge a decent score on a tricky pitch.

I found the stats advice helpful. It was never meant to replace the conclusions you make once you are actually batting – the experience you pick up over a career to gauge what a winning total can be on a certain type of pitch – it was just there to provide a basic guideline. Personally, it helped me focus and made sure we didn't leave too much to the final 'death' overs. We were never meant to follow it slavishly.

It pains me to see how history has been rewritten. We were a good ODI side. You don't get to number one in the world by luck. Losing that ICC Champions Trophy final has changed how we'll be remembered. I think we were better than that.

One of the things I learned was how quickly life could change. At the end of 2011, just before the last ODI against India, the England team's media manager, James Avery, asked if I would give an interview to CNN. No problem, I thought.

But the interview was all about the success we – and I – had enjoyed in the previous year. We were all due to attend the ICC's annual awards ceremony in London later that day and, for the first time, it crossed my mind that I might have won something.

I had been nominated a few weeks previously. But the other guys on the short list were Hashim Amla, Alastair Cook and Sachin Tendulkar and, with Hashim having flown across from South Africa for the dinner, I suspected he had been told he had won. It was such a strong list it felt an honour to be on it.

There was a sense within the team, though, that we might do pretty well this year. Cooky and I were both nominated for overall player of the year and the two of us were joined by Jimmy Anderson in the nominations for Test player of the year. Tim Bresnan was nominated for ODI performance of the year.

I was sitting on a table with Cooky when it was announced that he had won the award for Test player of the year. After that a floor manager came up to me and said that, if I won, I should walk up to the stage via the front steps and not those at the side. 'I think that might be a bit of a clue, Trotty,' Andy Flower chuckled.

Sure enough, my name was announced and I went up to receive the award, flustered by the attention and slightly embarrassed to have added my name to the list of winners (I was the first England player to win it outright, though Andrew Flintoff shared it with Jacques Kallis in 2005). Sachin had won it the previous year and Mitchell Johnson the year before that. Ricky Ponting had won it twice. It was pretty overwhelming to join such company. Five of us – me, Cooky, Jimmy, Swanny and Stuart Broad – were named in the ICC's Test team of the year. Swanny was named in the ODI side, too.

My sense of feeling overwhelmed clearly showed. During the press conference after the event, I used the word 'determinate' in an answer – I think I was unsure whether to say 'determined' or 'motivated' and came out with a hybrid of both – which gave Jimmy and Swanny, in particular, a good laugh.

Anyway, as I reflected on a pretty surreal evening, an incident came to mind. During the early summer of 2010, I had been driving down to London when I stopped into a service station on the M40 to buy some petrol.

As I stood in line to pay, I could see a copy of the *Cricketer* magazine on the racks beside me. I told myself not to look at it and tried to put it out of my mind. But I never was much good at resisting temptation and, before I left the shop, I decided to take a quick look.

The article was, I think, by Steve James – who is a very good journalist – and was about the players he thought would make up the Ashes squad to tour Australia at the end of the year. The sub-headline, as I remember it, was 'Is Jonathan Trott already England's forgotten man?' It went on to suggest that Ravi Bopara would soon be back in the side ahead of me. Bearing in mind that Steve and Andy Flower were pretty close, I figured there was probably some basis for the piece and knew I needed runs in the first Test if I was to play more than another game or two.

Now, here I was, named as the best player in the world over the last twelve months. I had already won the England player of the year award earlier in the 2011 season – again, I was probably competing with Alastair Cook for the award – and, with the England team recently recognised as the number one Test side in the world, it was lovely recognition of the contributions I had made to that achievement.

To put that in perspective, at the end of the 2009 English summer with my century on debut, I'd been the new star. Six months later I was a has-been, and twelve months after that I was a star again. It shows not just what a fickle game it can be, but how fickle those that judge us can be. You will, I think, therefore understand when I say that such awards – and such articles warning of your impending doom – start to be seen with a touch of cynicism. The criticism and the praise: you have to ignore them both if you want to perform at your best. They can both be equally damaging.

Kevin Pietersen:

What did Trotty bring to the side? He brought solidity to our top order. Whatever the situation, he exuded calm. Until Brisbane, when he went out to bat with tears in his eyes, I never worried about him. He would just go about his business in a quiet, unhurried manner that spread confidence throughout the dressing room. When he was at the other end, you felt he could withstand whatever was thrown at him and you would be able to see off the bowling and get on top of it. He had everything under control. He was the perfect teammate.

Trotty was England's rock. He was the man we relied

upon in a crisis, the man we knew would deliver when we needed him. I always felt I could relax before batting with him in the side as I knew he would be out there a while. It is no coincidence that, when our rock crumbled, our results deteriorated.

The day I was made one of Wisden's cricketers of the year was memorable, too. I've actually never read the piece about me included in the *Almanack* but the illustrious history of the publication – and the significance of an award that had previously been won by so many players I admired – wasn't lost on me. It was a thrill to be able to take my dad to the dinner in the Long Room at Lord's, where he sat next to Mike Brearley, a man we had both long admired and whose books we had read together when I was growing up. I was delighted to be able to repay my dad in that very small way for everything he had done for me. Those moments aren't the reason you play, but they are nice to look back on. I'm glad I was able to share it with my dad. He deserved that and much, much more.

I know a lot of sports people say this – and I'm not always sure I believe them, either – but those personal awards are actually not that important to many of us. That's not meant to sound ungrateful, but it is a team game and by that stage of my career I was completely focused on team success with Warwickshire and England. The ICC award – a slender, golden statue with a cricket ball at its top – is still in its box in an upstairs room of my house. It's not on display or anything like that. I don't even recall the last time I saw it.

But they aren't entirely meaningless. They are the little rewards along the way that remind you and your family that you have made progress or achieved something. They are a recognition of the part you have played in the team's success and, while it's not something I've ever thought too deeply about, maybe it is something I'll be able to look back on with pride in the years to come. Maybe my kids, too, will look at the trophy and take some pride in their dad's achievements. That's a nice thought.

9

2012
The Fall

I sn't it often the way that travelling in expectation is better than the reality of arriving?

That's the way it seemed with reaching number one in the Test rankings. It wasn't just that the moment we achieved it was underwhelming – for me, anyway – but that our period on top of the rankings was characterised by a succession of defeats. We had talked of it being the start of an era. In reality, it was over before it began. That cliché about it always being later than you think: there's a lot of truth in it.

My own theory is that, once we achieved our goal of reaching number one, we lost direction. We never replicated that moment at Loughborough where Nathan Leamon had sparked our imagination by detailing what was possible. We never refocused or readjusted our sights. We never united with a common goal in mind in quite the same way.

That's not to say we fell apart, or anything so dramatic or obvious. It was more that we lost our edge. We lost that single-minded determination that had helped drive us on. We became just a little bit rudderless. We were less a team and more a group of individuals who had been picked to do a similar job.

The problem was that our loss of focus coincided with a period when many of us were starting to feel the miles on the clock. If we weren't struggling physically – and many of the guys were – we were starting to struggle mentally. The relentless demands of the schedule and the intensity of the way we were managed made it very hard to sustain success over a long period of time. If you keep a plant in a hothouse you may accelerate its growth, but you may also accelerate its death.

What we should have done, I think, is aim to become a great side. We should have looked at the points gained in the Test championship by the great teams of the past and tried to emulate and surpass them. So, by the time the series against India finished, we were on about 124 rankings points. While that probably sounds meaningless to most people, if you look at the graph of historic rankings, you can see that the benchmark of a great team – and I'm talking the Australian team of the early part of the century and the West Indies team of the late seventies and early eighties – is at least 130 points. Instead that rating of 124 became our high water mark.

And we should have realised that an experienced team needs to be treated just a little differently to a young and inexperienced team. We needed a little more space to breathe and a little less intensity around the set-up. Most of all, we needed some time off.

Andy Flower:

The point of the targets was to challenge the team. We wanted to show them how world-class teams performed and the standards they set.

But Trotty is right. We didn't reset our sights once we made it to number one in the Test rankings. Instead of building on that achievement, we floundered. We were looking for something to chase after but, while we were looking, we were in limbo.

I'm not sure that was the case specifically in the UAE. On that occasion we just played the spin bowling really badly. You could understand it, to some extent, against Ajmal as he was a top-class bowler. But Rehman wasn't that quality and we played him as if he were a world-beater.

Trotty actually made a strong case for how we should refocus ourselves based upon statistics and achieving some of the things the great teams had achieved, but some of the other players were never really motivated by those things and it didn't take hold.

It's true that the character of the team did change a bit with success. Maybe there was a little loss of focus or maybe the focus fell on other things away from cricket. But I noticed it and it scared me.

Intrinsic motivation is nearly always more beneficial in sport. But as we enjoyed more success, it became clear that we had a few players motivated more extrinsically.

> The character of a team is never constant. You always
> have to evolve and improve. We probably didn't do that
> as effectively as I would have liked. To someone as driven
> as Trotty, that probably was a frustration.

It is one of the great truisms of cricket that winning makes everything OK. So, during that period when we had been rising through the rankings, there were few fall-outs in the dressing room. Once we started losing, though, the divisions which had always been there became more apparent. Tensions rose and splits grew. Almost exactly twelve months after we received the ICC Test mace – awarded to the number one side – our captain retired, our best batsman was suspended and we lost the ranking after defeat to South Africa.

It may be relevant that we were not an especially young side when we went to the top of the rankings. The same experience that had helped us reach the top may have contributed to our decline. Tim Bresnan, who had done as good a job as anyone as third seamer, had an elbow problem that robbed him of a bit of nip. KP's knee started to bother him, Matt Prior had tendon trouble and it became apparent that Graeme Swann's elbow would require management. None of them were helped by our relentless schedule.

The moment we reached number one – with the defeat of India at Edgbaston in 2011 – was actually a bit of an anti-climax.

Well, for me, at least. I had injured my shoulder in the field at Trent Bridge and missed the final two Tests of the series. I was at the games but, what with all the media requirements and not making it on to the pitch, I felt a bit separated from the achievement.

Those media and sponsorship requirements were onerous. At The Oval, when we were all together and wanted time to reflect on what we had achieved, we were torn apart by the endless requests for interviews and appearances.

Everyone understands those things are important. Everyone understands that those commitments are the reason we are well paid. But it was a shame that the moment was lost amid the need to fulfil our other duties.

Not that any of us saw the significance at the time. At the time, we thought it would be the start of an era. We thought we had the talent, work ethic and relative youth to go on and achieve a spell of several years at the top.

It wasn't to be. We lost our next four Tests and won only one of our next four series. Several of the team were much closer to the end of their international careers than any of us realised. I guess not many climbers linger for long on top of Everest, but it would have been nice to stay a while more.

After victory against India in the summer of 2011, we had a relatively long break ahead of our next Test series. We needed it, too. We had been on the go for a long time and we needed time to decompress. Our next series, against Pakistan in the UAE, was not until the start of 2012.

There are a lot of theories about what went wrong on that tour from our perspective, but the most obvious factor was that Pakistan performed very well. They outplayed us at our own attritional game. They were almost unrecognisable from the rabble – yes, they'd been talented in 2010, but they were divided and diluted by corruption and poor discipline – that we had defeated in England eighteen months earlier.

Somehow we never got going on that tour to the UAE. It's an odd thing but, unlike every other country we visited, there was almost no cricket culture in the UAE. Wherever else you go, it is significant news. You can feel the buzz. People stop you in the street, waiters ask you about it and it feels like an event.

It's not like that in the UAE. In the UAE, where Pakistan currently play their home games due to security concerns in their homeland, cricket is an irrelevance. The only people interested are expats and not many of them have the time or inclination to come to the Tests. As a consequence, there was an oddly flat feel to the whole series and we were never able to shake ourselves into life.

That's not an excuse – it must have been even harder for Pakistan – but we never seemed to get going.

Andrew Strauss:

We said all the right things when we became world number one. We were serious about staying there and in no way did we take the tour to the UAE lightly.

But when I look back, we could have used getting to number one as an opportunity to refresh what we did. We could have used it to take a new look at what we were doing and see how we could improve. Instead we tried

to stick with what we did. We were consciously trying to
perpetuate what we had done before rather than striving
to improve, which is actually how we had always been
in the past. As a result, we may have cruised a bit. In
retrospect, that was a mistake.

We were reluctant to change methods that had worked for
us in the past. So we went into that first Test in Dubai with
the same balance of attack – three seamers and a spinner –
that had worked for us in England and Australia. It meant
that Broad and Anderson both bowled thirty overs in the
first innings and we played Chris Tremlett ahead of Monty
Panesar.

We were a bit complacent, I think. Pakistan had been
such a mess a couple of years earlier and, since then, had
lost three of their best players due to the match-fixing bans.
We said all the right things and we worked hard but, on a
level, we thought we could beat them pretty comfortably.

Having said that, few of us thought that Saaed Ajmal
would prove such a threat. I had found him relatively
straightforward in England. He is quite short so he didn't
gain a huge amount of bounce. He tended to bowl a bit
shorter than most spinners, so I played him largely off the
back foot and used his pace to my advantage. I think he
only dismissed me once in my Test career, and that was in
the final Test of that series when I top-edged a slog-sweep
off a doosra.

But on the low pitches of the UAE, the stumps were
always in play. Unless you could pick him – I could, but
I noticed a few couldn't – you were in real trouble as the

ball would skid on and beat you on either edge. Abdur Rehman, the left-arm spinner who bowled at an unusually sharp pace, was a handful, too. He bowled a tight line, turned the ball just enough to threaten the edge and, with natural variation making it hard to know whether the ball would turn or go straight on, he punished any errors.

I didn't really buy into the idea that we had an obvious weakness against spin. Not in the Test team, anyway. Those two were terrific bowlers operating in conditions that suited them. Any team would have struggled. Yes, we lost the first Test in Sri Lanka, too, but we were on the wrong end of an important toss in that game and we did win the next one. By the end of the year, we had beaten India on pitches tailor-made for their spinners.

Complacency was more of an issue. We were complacent in the UAE even after we lost. The first Test was dismissed as a blip and we arguably should have won the second and third. We were set only 145 to win in the second, in Abu Dhabi, but were bowled out for 72, while in the final Test in Dubai we bowled them out for 99 in the first innings. You shouldn't lose a Test from that position.

Then we smashed them in the limited-overs games and the cracks were papered over. We were still number one in the rankings and the need to reflect on our failings and confront our issues abated. Andy was definitely pushing us harder than ever, but we never sat down and discussed a change of approach. We fooled ourselves into thinking we were unlucky with the conditions, the DRS, the questionable action of Saeed Ajmal and a couple of poor sessions. We put that together and convinced ourselves we didn't have a problem. It was, in retrospect, a major mistake.

We defeated West Indies comfortably enough at home at the start of our summer, but South Africa was always going to be a tougher challenge. Again, they won nearly all the key moments and, after winning the first Test, made it 2–0 in the third when we were chasing an unlikely target. We dropped some catches and, from a position of 170 for one on the first day at The Oval, failed to establish the game-defining platform we should have done. We didn't do ourselves justice in that series.

Losing was one thing. The real issue was the disintegration of our carefully cultivated team spirit as the summer wore on.

At some point between the first Test and the second, the relationship between KP and several other members of the side took a sharp dip. There had been tensions and differences for a while but it was after he suspected that several members of the team were involved in sending tweets from a parody account – KP Genius – that things really deteriorated.

At first, KP tried to play along. He even retweeted a couple, I believe. But, as it went on and they gained an audience, his attitude changed. And, with the tweets mocking his perceived arrogance but also betraying the odd nugget that suggested a little inside knowledge, he started to believe that someone inside the dressing room was involved.

It really upset him. He felt he was being mocked by people inside the team and, when he expressed his concerns to the team management, they were brushed aside.

To this day, I don't know the truth of what went on. I don't know if some of our teammates were involved – though it would be astonishingly unprofessional if they were – and I don't know if he should have let it consume him to the extent that it did. For me – and the likes of Ian Bell and Alastair Cook, who were equally immune to the charms of Twitter – the whole episode was an avoidable distraction. It was an example of people allowing themselves to be drawn into a world that should have been an irrelevance. It was an example of us moving away from the basics – working hard, concentrating on our games and our goals – and allowing the outside world into the dressing room.

Why did any of us feel the need to be on Twitter? I don't know. For me it was a case of ego creeping into the dressing room. Being recognised as good cricketers wasn't enough for everyone any more. Some people wanted to be celebrities or to use their status for financial gain. All of that is understandable; it is a short career, after all. But when it starts to detract from the day job – which was our cricket – then you have a problem. I still think it was an unnecessary distraction.

I didn't know the extent of KP's anger until after the game at Leeds. I was completely occupied with trying to get things right on the pitch and hadn't picked up on the growing tension within the dressing room. But following the game, in which he thrashed a ridiculous century and was named man of the match, he went into the press conference and said something along the lines of it 'not being easy being him' in the England dressing room and hinted that the next Test might be his last. Then the issue with the BlackBerry messages became apparent and the fault lines widened.

The incident hardly requires retelling but, in case there is anyone out there who does not recall what happened, it transpired that KP had been exchanging messages with some of our South African opponents in which he had been less than complimentary about Andrew Strauss. He never meant them to become public – and he may well feel a bit let down by those friends in the South Africa side that they were revealed – but they didn't look good and, in an England dressing room that respected their captain enormously, they went down very, very badly.

I actually think that, when he reflects on his life in cricket, this will be the incident that KP most regrets. Much of the time his fault, if that is the way you want to term it, was his honesty. He has never learned when it is wise to say nothing; never learned – and it is a typically English characteristic – to say something vague and non-committal rather than expressing his honest view. That can come across as blunt or brash, but he is, from his point of view, a very honest man. He has a lot more in common with Geoff Boycott than either of them would care to admit.

But I know that KP, like all of us, both liked and respected Andrew Strauss very much. He knew what an excellent captain Straussy had been and he knew that, after a fine career with the bat, he was struggling. They had been through a lot together and he never wanted to overshadow the end of Straussy's international career with this petty squabble. He deserved a great deal better and KP knew it.

As a player who just wanted to get his head down and do his job, I found the entire episode a distraction we could have done without while trying to beat the best side in the world. Sadly, we seemed more competitive in our own dressing room than we were on the pitch.

There had been issues for a while. There was some resentment about KP's involvement with the IPL and his desire to play a little less international cricket. There had been talk all summer about the next central contracts and KP was keen to play much less ODI cricket – perhaps none at all – while carrying on as a member of the T20 side. The ECB were insisting he made himself available for both formats or neither. Maybe a few were jealous of the money he was earning; maybe they just felt he had allowed his head to be turned from the priority: winning games for England. But most players, given the opportunity to earn the sums KP could in the IPL, would have taken it. In fact public opinion has now changed so much that it seems players are actively encouraged to take part in such overseas leagues, with the England team management acknowledging the benefits of the experience.

Anyway, as a result of the BlackBerry messages, KP was dropped ahead of the final Test. We lost the series – and our number one status – and Straussy retired in a slightly sad way. Instead of all the focus of his final Test being on his tremendous career, it was on a fall-out with a player which perhaps contributed to our defeat. There was resentment towards KP in the dressing room and it really did seem that he wouldn't play for us again.

That KP was recalled owed almost everything to Alastair Cook. Having been appointed captain, Cooky was adamant that he wanted to take the strongest possible team to India. He had to persuade Andy Flower, but there wasn't much doubt in the dressing room that a team with KP in it was stronger than a team without him.

As part of the 'reintegration' process, we all had to have meetings with him in a hotel in Oxford. For me, at least, it was a slightly surreal experience. We had never fallen out, so I came into the room, saw there was a moderator there and laughed. 'How you doing, KP?' I asked. 'Yeah, good, Trotty,' he replied. And then we both laughed. The whole situation reminded me of school. KP had basically been asked to stand in the corner for a bit.

He was good in India; ridiculously good in Mumbai. And he tried pretty hard to pull things back with the rest of the team. It was fine, really.

But something had changed. Maybe it was just the departure of Straussy, maybe there was some lasting resentment, or maybe we were all just a little more weary. But we never quite recaptured the spirit that we had known in the past, the unity of purpose and direction that had taken us to the top. It was still brilliant, but it maybe wasn't quite as much fun. It didn't feel as if we had the bond we once had.

We enjoyed successes after that UAE tour – notably in India – but they were built more on individual brilliance than the same relentlessly strong team performances.

Take that 2012 tour of India: after being thrashed in the first Test in Ahmedabad, Alastair Cook and KP played two great innings and our spinners bowled very well to help us win in Mumbai. The rest of us? We might as well have stayed in bed. It wasn't the same as it had been against India in England or Australia in Australia. On those occasions, everyone in the team combined to wear down our opposition. We were relentless and consistent.

Maybe Andy had changed a bit by then, too. Or our attitude to him had changed. But during that India tour, Andy told us he was going to relinquish control of the limited-overs sides. The idea was that, after several years immersed in the team, he would take a step back and allow himself more time for family life. He would remain as head coach of all the England teams, but Ashley Giles would take day-to-day charge of the white ball squads.

Which all sounds fine, doesn't it? Everyone could see the sense of spreading the load and maybe, with different characters involved, sharing the coaching could have worked well.

But Andy couldn't accept it. I'm not at all convinced that his heart was ever in the decision and it soon became apparent that he wasn't able to let go sufficiently to allow Ash to do his job as he would have liked. Andy would turn up at games when nobody expected him and generally lurked in the background in a way that made Ash's life harder than it might have been.

Part of the problem was the different styles of the two men. Neither was necessarily right or wrong, but after years of Andy's hard, driven approach, Ashley's lighter touch felt like a breath of fresh air. His coaching style was more matey, more gentle, more patient, more approachable. It made Andy's approach – the energy, the drive, the intensity, the calculated impatience – appear all the more abrasive. Going from the relative fun of the limited-overs squad to the intensity of the Test dressing room under Andy felt like going back to work after a holiday.

Ashley Giles:

I think the split coaching role probably did cause a few issues. If I had my time again, I wouldn't accept the job in those circumstances. I think I would probably have to insist on control of the team, pick my own support team and have no interference. That's not to say there was anything the matter with the support team I had, but it's always easier if you pick your own.

My impression was that the set-up was, by that stage, a bit tense. For a guy like Trotty – a guy who really appreciates clarity and certainty – I think it probably was a bit unsettling.

It all unravelled pretty quickly at the end. He went home, Swanny retired, KP was dropped and within weeks, me and Andy were gone, too.

It was probably relevant that Ash had played with several of the team. He knew the likes of KP, Cooky, Jimmy, me and Belly very well before he started so there was a natural ease within the relationships. It wasn't that he was soft – in terms of discipline and work ethic he was identical to

Andy and there was certainly a line that we could not cross – but more that he knew when to push and when to back off. He valued time off and freshness more than Andy, whose reaction to most challenges was to plough through and work harder – and encouraged an easy, communicative relationship.

Andy resisted such a relationship. Although, as a player, he had been a great teammate to those around him, he had a theory that, as a coach, he needed to keep a certain distance from the team. He created a boundary between us. He was seen a little as you might a head teacher at school. I don't think I ever had dinner with him in the entire period he was England coach. He seemed to equate easing up with weakness.

I fear that Andy was offended by the way he saw us react to Ash. He saw the enjoyment, heard the laughter and seemed to take it as a personal slight. When the limited-overs games were over, and with all his energy now directed towards the Test team, he would drive us harder than ever when the Test squad got back together. It was as if he were angry with having had to relinquish power and felt the need to reassert his authority at every opportunity.

And the more he pushed us, the more we pulled away from him. The methods that might have worked when we were all young and innocent and hungry and united started to cause resentment. What once had seemed fresh now seemed stale and, for a team with a lot of miles in their legs, it was all a bit much. We needed, at that stage, a bit more carrot and a bit less stick.

Andy Flower:

In retrospect, the split coaching was a mistake. It's true that I wasn't entirely convinced I wanted to step back from the full-time role. I was still hungry for success and I still felt there was unfinished business. I didn't want to do it, but I had to. Maybe that was a factor. I did it for family reasons and clearly those things are important.

I think we could both have handled the situation a bit better. I like Ashley. I rate him as a coach and a man. We wanted the same thing and we both tried our best. We both went into it with the best of intentions. But there were tensions and there were some differences. I suppose I was a bit tougher on discipline and his environment was a bit more relaxed.

It didn't work out. I think he felt I was not allowing him to do the job his own way – I'm not sure I would accept that suggestion, but I suppose I can see where he was coming from – and I felt we had different leadership styles and coaching philosophies. I can see why someone like Trotty would feel the situation was less clear than it had been.

Some things were just misunderstandings. There were times when we had to rest players and, while that was probably a frustration to him, he would understand that it was necessary at times and would have done the same thing.

I think that split-coaching role can work. If there is greater disparity between the playing squads – and there is more now than there was when Ash and I were in the roles – then it could work. And if the situation is

really well co-ordinated by the managing director of the
England teams – the person in Andrew Strauss's job – and
both coaches buy into the same philosophy, then it can
work, too.

It worked in a slightly different way when we had three
captains, one for each of the formats. The management
team was the same the whole way through that period,
so the messages were the same and the expectations were
the same.

I feel for Ashley. When he was handed the team at
the end of the Ashes tour in early 2014, confidence and
energy levels were low. It was a difficult situation for him.

I have wondered many times what would have happened
if I'd spoken to Ash, not Andy, ahead of the limited-overs
series against Australia at the end of the 2013 summer.
Had it been Ash, I might well have felt a little more able
to express my concerns about playing and let him know
how much I was struggling. I might have been able to ask
for that series off and benefited from the break ahead of
the Ashes tour.

As it was, Andy did mention that I could have a break
if required. But, as he said it, he pointed out that I had
already missed the ODI series against India at the start of
the year, the inference being that I really should play this
series. I expect, had I opened up to him, that he would
have been understanding because, at heart, he is a great,
caring guy. But he didn't always seem that approachable,
so I let myself be led into the series. Ultimately, I have to
take responsibility for that mistake.

That's not meant to sound like a criticism of Andy. I consider myself fortunate to have worked with both him and Ash and he was the driving force behind our success. If he asked me, I would run through a wall for him today. But the one thing a player wants more than anything from their coaching staff is clarity and consistency. Having two voices in the dressing room only works if they have the same message and, for a while, Ash and Andy didn't.

The other issue was that, a couple of months after KP had been told he couldn't have his workload reduced, Flower was doing just that. You can imagine how Kevin saw that. He probably had a point, too. A couple of years on and the England management are keen to rest players and encourage all but a few to specialise in either the white-ball or the red-ball format.

Again, to be fair to Andy, I'm not sure he wanted to relinquish any control at all. He said that he had family reasons and it would be wrong to speculate on someone's personal life. It wasn't as if he just fancied a bit more time off.

By the time the 2013 Ashes series came round we were all living off memory. The magic, the freshness, the energy had all gone. It didn't feel as if we were trying to climb; it felt as if we were trying not to fall. We were still, in many ways, the same team that had reached number one but most of us carried the scars of all the fights we had endured to get there. We had just enough to hang on for victory, but it was pretty clear that, as a team, we were coming to the end of our life span.

Andy Flower:

When we won in 2010–11 in Australia, we were desperate for success. It had been more than twenty years since England had won an Ashes series in Australia and it had been our goal for a long time. It was a special achievement and everyone involved wanted it badly.

But by 2013–14, we had enjoyed a lot of success together. The sense was more that it would be lovely if we won again, but we didn't want it with the same passion as we had a few years earlier. Australia wanted it more than us. They had been starved of success for so long. They were the desperate team.

Tiredness was a big part of the problem. The team were drained. We all were. The scrutiny really gets to you after a while and I'm not sure people always realise how much effort, how much energy and how much concentration goes into playing in a winning side.

The schedule was crazy. Absolutely ridiculous. I didn't want to say anything about it at the time as I didn't want to be seen to be making excuses. Australia played better than us and they deserved the credit for winning. But it was a terrible idea to play back-to-back Ashes series and playing the second one in Australia was, I believe, an advantage to them. Mitchell Johnson bowled very well and he was brilliantly captained by Michael Clarke.

Graeme Swann, for so long the fulcrum of that team, still finished that 2013 Ashes series as our highest wicket-taker but you could tell he was in decline. The control he offered, the drift and dip and turn he gained, had played a huge role in helping us up the rankings. Having stood at slip to him, I rate him as highly as any spinner I faced. At his best, he was a terrific bowler.

He was still good in 2013. But he had lost a bit of snap, a bit of energy. The dip was a little more gradual, the drift a little less pronounced. We seemed to prepare pitches that were designed to help him and the burden on him – we were still playing a four-man attack – probably didn't do anything to increase his long-term career prospects. He had already undergone surgery on his right elbow.

As that summer wore on, an incident from a few years earlier kept playing on my mind. It occurred on the second day of the Melbourne Test at the end of 2010 – the day I scored a century and Australia realised they were going to lose the Ashes once more – when you might have thought I would be absorbed in my own thoughts.

But on that day, Ricky Ponting lost his temper with Aleem Dar when a decision went against Australia. The Australians had appealed for a caught behind off KP when he was on 49; I was at the bowler's end. Aleem didn't give it and the television reviews backed him. But Ricky couldn't accept it; he completely lost it and was eventually fined 40 per cent of his match fee.

It wasn't just that setback that had contributed to Ricky's outburst, though. He had been struggling all series. Twice he had been caught down the leg side; once he had fallen to an incredible catch. He just couldn't get a break as a batsman, his side were losing and it was beginning to wear him down.

He was a batsman I had always admired. It wasn't just his talent, but his calm and his confidence. Now here he was, an undisputed great of the game, reduced to an ill-chosen argument with a very good umpire as the pressure and disappointment ate away at him. The game spares nobody, I thought. It was an odd conclusion to reach midway through one of the best innings of my career, but the moment stuck with me. I knew, even in that triumphant moment, that the same fate awaited me. The game spares nobody.

Andy Flower:

Could we get together in twenty or thirty years and celebrate a great period for the national team? I'd like to believe we could, yes. There has been acrimony and the divides have been large, but time can heal.

10

BARBADOS, MAY 2015
Part 2

It took one ball in Antigua. One ball on my return to Test cricket for me to realise my return wasn't going to work out. One ball to realise there would be no fairytale ending.

The delivery from Jerome Taylor was full – almost a full toss – and on my legs. At my best, I should have clipped it for four. Below my best, I should have turned it down to fine leg for a single. It was the sort of ball that I should have been dreaming of receiving.

But I was miles away from it.

So poor was my balance, so uncontrolled my movement that I had walked down the pitch and turned, in horror, to see the ball miss my leg stump by millimetres.

I couldn't believe where I had found myself. A full metre down the pitch. A full stride outside off stump. It was shocking.

This was exactly what had happened in Australia. The nightmare was returning.

I know what you're thinking. Give yourself some time; it's one ball; there were bound to be nerves; give yourself a break.

But I couldn't. I couldn't catch my breath. I couldn't control my mind. I couldn't block out the distractions and focus on batting. And now, here I was, out in the middle and trapped in a situation that I knew would end badly. It was a terrible moment.

I tried reminding myself of Steve's words. I tried not to catastrophise the situation. But it didn't seem as if I had any time to collect myself. I couldn't stop the intrusion of the negative thoughts. I recalled Ricky Ponting, the great batsman I so admired, reflecting on his career and talking about that 'little voice that sits on an athlete's shoulder as they compete'. It is a negative voice, he had said. 'One that says you're no good, that you can't win, that it's not worth it, that you should give up. I couldn't get rid of the little bastard at the end.' I knew what he meant.

One of my coaches – I can't remember which one – told me that the definition of concentration was the absence of irrelevant thoughts. Whereas on debut at The Oval it had been easy to concentrate on the ball and block out the distractions, here it was exactly the other way around. Irrelevant thoughts were all I had.

I had been fine going into the game. I had been fine putting on my pads. I was hoping we would bat first so I could get out there and show people what I could do.

I had enjoyed Antigua. We were staying in a great

location – opposite Jolly Beach – and I had enjoyed water-skiing and being back in the England environment. I felt calm and confident.

But somehow, when I crossed the boundary rope, everything changed. The volume increased, the speed of events increased, my movements became jerky and exaggerated. I couldn't find the bubble I used to climb inside to block out the distractions and concentrate on the ball. There was so much going on and I was noticing all of it.

Falling over on to the off side had always been a weakness in my batting. I knew I was at my best when I hit the ball straight; I knew I was struggling when I missed out on my legs. But when gripped by anxiety, all the movements became sharp and accentuated. I wasn't able to control them. I felt myself moving and I couldn't stop.

All the time I used to have to play the ball had disappeared. Suddenly it was on me before I was ready. I'd had my eyes checked, so I knew they weren't the problem. The issue was that my head was moving so much at the point of delivery, I wasn't giving myself a chance to pick up the length. I knew that, but I couldn't stop moving.

I reverted to the method I'd used for so long – scratching my guard to buy myself some time and help me clear my mind. Even as I did it, though, I was thinking, 'This isn't working.' I could still hear the crowd; I could still hear the West Indies players; I could still see all those faces in the press box judging me and about to find me wanting. I couldn't block any of it out.

If there was a bright side, it was that my suffering was brief. I was out by the end of the first over of the game. My comeback innings had lasted three balls and produced no runs. All the moments of hard work and anguish. For that.

Kevin Pietersen:

I played in the Caribbean Premier League not long after that tour. Stuart Williams, who had been the West Indies team's assistant coach, told me that Trotty was the one wicket they really wanted in that series. They knew that, if they let him get back to his best, he would hold England together and provide the platform for those big totals that were a feature of our cricket during the years we made it to number one in the world. They talked about him as one of the greatest England players of recent years.

The West Indies were right, too. If Trotty had rediscovered his form and confidence on that tour, England would have won. In the only Test he did score runs – in Grenada – they did win. England needed his solidity. They had a young side and needed someone to build the platform at the top of the innings.

I wish Trotty could have heard how much they rated him. I wish he could have had the belief in his ability that they had. But, by then, I think he had lost confidence in himself to a chronic extent. He was so tightly trapped inside his own battle – trying so hard to keep out the negative voices – that he couldn't hear the positive ones.

It was a good ball. It was on off stump, it forced a stroke and it nipped away. I might have edged it to slip when

I was well set and at my best. Jerome Taylor is a terrific bowler. He's probably bowled about twenty-five balls at me in my career and he's dismissed me four times.

But I knew it wasn't going to work out. I knew that, for all the work we had done in getting me to that stage, for all the improvements I had made in my attitude as a player and as a person, something was different now. There was too much scarring.

Andrew Strauss:

I didn't think there was any way back for him after Brisbane, to be honest.

When someone has suffered an experience like that, you want to ease them back in a low-profile, low-pressure environment. But that doesn't exist in international cricket: the opposition want to take advantage of any perceived weakness and the media will scrutinise every move. It's such an unforgiving environment. It's all or nothing.

My advice at the time was: forget England. Just get to a stage where you're enjoying your cricket again with Warwickshire and don't look beyond that.

To fight his way back into contention was incredible. He had to dig so deep to do so; he had to challenge himself in ways he had never challenged himself before. He had to conquer his demons and put himself back in the line of fire despite all his fears and anxiety. It's heroic.

He deserved a better ending. He deserves to be recognised for what he has achieved. His individual achievements are phenomenal and he played a big part in the success of an England team that was number one in the world in Test and ODI cricket.

In some ways, his role was unglamorous. He would run from fine leg to fine leg. He would blunt the new ball and see the bowlers off at their most fresh. He would set the platform in ODI cricket and let others play the big shots.

But he would have done anything for that England side. He lived and breathed it for several years. He became a great team man and I hope it's that Jonathan Trott that people remember.

What do I mean by that? Well, the first time I played Test cricket, I had no idea about everything that went with it. I had no idea about the media, I had never heard of Twitter and there was pretty much no expectation. I went into it full of confidence and with no fear.

This time, the innocence was gone. Even as I watched Alastair Cook take the first ball of that match, I could see the faces up in the media centre and I knew what they would be talking about, imagined how they would slaughter me if I failed. I'd just had five months of abuse – not only in the media, but from people making faces on the street – but also so much support that I felt I was carrying the hopes of my friends and family on my shoulders. Yes, that had always been there, but now I knew all the consequences of success and failure. I knew all the pain of defeat and how much it took to be successful. It hit me only once I was out there: I couldn't do it any more.

I could make a thousand excuses. I could say that it

A special moment: with Lily after The Oval Test of 2013. The Ashes were ours once more. But I had been in tears that morning and I had to go straight to Leeds for the start of the ODI series. The relentlessness of the schedule was weighing heavy by that stage. *(Gareth Copley/Getty Images)*

In the nets with Ashley Giles at Leeds during the 2013 ODI series. He had always known what made me tick and, by this stage, we both knew I had a serious problem. *(Stu Forster/Getty Images)*

Hanging out with some celebrity fans at Leeds. *(Philip Brown)*

Fielding on the boundary in Australia was quite an experience. The crowds there are more hostile than anywhere else in the world. *(Philip Brown)*

After the Brisbane Test in 2013. I knew I was going home and was pretty sure my career was over. David Warner had accused me of backing away from Mitchell Johnson and having scared eyes. I wanted to look him straight in the eyes when I said 'Well played.' He didn't have the balls to look me in the eye. *(Philip Brown)*

Jonathan Trott: I wasn't suffering from depression, I was just burnt out

14 March 2014

England players will be asked if they want Jonathan Trott to return to international set up

17 March 2014

It will be difficult for any England captain to trust Jonathan Trott again

14 March 2014

ECB left exposed by cases of Jonathan Trott and Kevin Pietersen

20 March 2014

Jonathan Trott must accept team-mates and opponents will feel he did a runner

16 March 2014

A selection of headlines from the *Telegraph* following my Sky interview. I felt as if they were trying to destroy me.

Waiting to bat in a second team match against Yorkshire in 2014. A long, long way from the Gabba or Lord's.

The Lord's final against Durham, September 2014. A proud day, too. I had scored half-centuries in the quarter- and semi-finals in my comeback season, and was actually enjoying the pressure and expectation of the day. I felt ready to return to Test cricket. *(Philip Brown)*

A proud moment. I'd just been awarded my fiftieth cap and I'd made it back to Test cricket. I consider that one of my greatest achievements. And I was walking out to open the batting with one of my great friends. But, as we stepped over the boundary, I realised I was in trouble. I couldn't cut out the distractions. Suddenly I felt all those eyes in the press box looking down on me and scrutinising my every move. *(Michael Steele/Getty Images)*

Walking off for the last time in Test cricket. I was in two minds, really. I wanted to soak up the sights and sounds of a Test for the last time, but I always wanted to get back to the dark of the dressing room. I was relieved it was all over, too. The Barmy Army gave me a nice ovation. I appreciated that. *(Michael Steele/Getty Images)*

There are 75 Test centuries between this quartet of England players. If Cooky were in the picture, that number would be well over 100. I know our period at the top was brief and some of our achievements have been overshadowed by arguments, but I hope people remember what a good side we were. *(Philip Brown)*

Abi took this picture of me at Turtle Bay as news of my retirement broke in Barbados. I had forgotten to turn my phone off and apparently it rang constantly. But I was mentally exhausted and slept through it.

My two biggest fans: Lily and Lexi.

I loved playing for England. My career didn't end the way I would have liked and there were some hard times along the way, but I feel hugely honoured to have represented England and I'm very proud of what our team achieved. There are many more good memories than bad. *(Philip Brown)*

might have been different if we had fielded first and I'd had some time to ease into my return. I could say that I wasn't prepared to open the batting and that, back in my more familiar position of number three, life might have been easier. I could claim that the warm-up period ahead of the Tests wasn't adequate.

But that's all irrelevant. If I'm honest, I think that, at my best, I could have coped with all those things. To flourish at Test level, you have to be able to cope with change and distraction. You have to block it out and find a way to succeed. There are no excuses. I just wasn't the player I used to be.

Nobody ever asked me if I fancied opening the batting. But it had become apparent when the squad was announced that, if there was to be a way back into the team, it was going to have to be as an opening batsman. Gary Ballance and Joe Root had done a great job at numbers three and four and deserved to stay there. Adam Lyth was a specialist opening batsman and I figured he and I would be competing for the chance to open with Alastair Cook.

If I'm honest, I had always wanted to bat at number four. I felt the move to number three had forced me to curb my more instinctive game and, once I got into the habit of playing there, I struggled to rediscover the fluency I had enjoyed earlier in my career. I'd always believed the demands of the positions varied more than some people thought, with the number three required to leave a lot more deliveries and display greater patience. But I've no complaints: number three was where the vacancy arose and, like any batsman, you would rather play slightly out of position than not play at all.

The first hint I had that I was in pole position to open in the Caribbean was when the team for the first tour game against a St Kitts side was announced and I was told I was opening. Great; I felt I knew what was needed and I'd be at the other end from my old friend, Cooky.

I was happy by the end of the first day of that tour game, too. They were modest opposition but, after we had bowled them out for 59, Cooky and I put on 158 for the first wicket before I was out for 72. I knew the bowling would get much tougher, but I was satisfied to have spent some time in the middle and gained what I think of as batting rhythm.

But then, with the team management unhappy about the quality of the St Kitts team, everything was changed. The teams were muddled up so that theirs contained a few of our players and, instead of playing a real game, we were very obviously involved in a practice match.

I hated these arrangements. It had happened several times before with England – first in Bangladesh, when I lost a first-class century after a game was degraded to allow us to field more than eleven players – and while I could understand the logic, I didn't think they ever proved beneficial.

All I wanted from these games was stability and clarity. But as soon as a game is robbed of its first-class status, as soon as it is made thirteen a side, as soon as the consequences for losing your wicket are removed, all the intensity is sucked from the games and they are reduced to something of a farce. It's no coincidence that, ahead of the 2010–11 Ashes, we played three really tough first-class games – mini-Tests, in a way – before starting the Test series. It enabled us to play the innings we did in Brisbane.

In that St Kitts game, the team management clearly wanted me to bat as many times as possible. But in those circumstances, with nothing resting on the game and an artificial atmosphere, I was never going to be able to get back into the bubble. Having batted fine in the first innings, I then failed twice – once due to a freak dismissal where a ball ballooned off my thigh pad to the keeper and once when I nicked one from Jimmy Anderson – and left the island with my confidence a little lower than it need have been.

Still, I'd earned that much-delayed fiftieth Test cap in Antigua. It was the same Test in which Jimmy earned his 100th cap and we were both presented with them by Nasser Hussain before the game. Nasser made an excellent speech to the lads in which he spoke of the sacrifices he'd had to make to enjoy a successful career in the game.

'We've one guy here who has given a lot and sacrificed a lot,' Nasser said, gesturing towards Jimmy. 'And we've one who may have given too much.' We all knew he was talking about me and I appreciated that he understood how hard it had been to get back to that level. He is one of the commentators who has never forgotten how hard it is to be a player.

It's not that way with everyone. On the morning of the second Test in Grenada, I woke early and checked my phone. I wanted to change my fantasy football side so I was using the Sky Sports app. I had no intention of checking the sports news, but there was a huge and unavoidable headline at the top of the page: 'Botham thinks it's time for Trott to be dropped.'

After one Test? I was pretty disappointed by that. Sir Ian is clearly a legend of the game, but I would have hoped he might remember how hard it can be at times and might have valued the consistency of selection that has been a feature of the more successful England side in recent years.

I did OK in that second Test. Jerome Taylor missed out with a shoulder injury, which made life much easier, so Cooky and I were able to put on 125 for the opening wicket. It was a slow pitch so we weren't exactly fluent, but it was England's first century opening stand in Test cricket for just over two years and it felt as if we'd laid a pretty decent platform.

Aware – far more aware than I should have been – that there would be complaints about our rate of scoring, I was out for 59 as I tried to push on. It was unnecessary, really, but Joe Root came in and made a brilliant century and it was satisfying to play a part in a rare away victory.

Just for a moment, when I pushed a drive back past Kemar Roach to the long-on boundary, I felt something familiar flicker within me; a sense of control and confidence. A sense that I could still do this. But it was an echo of a previous era. An encore at the end of a performance. A flashback to the younger, stronger batsman I used to be. I knew it was over.

If it seems odd to have decided that I was finished even while making a half-century, it is because I was out there long enough to understand. Despite batting for three and a half hours in that innings, I never regained the sense of focus I had once taken for granted. I never climbed back into the zone in which I used to bat. It was like waking from a dream; you might want to settle back into it, but there's no way.

I wondered if I might have lost a bit of hunger, too. My whole life until a few months earlier had been focused on succeeding in these moments. It was absolutely how I defined myself. But now I had understood that I wasn't a cricketer, cricket was something I did. I still enjoyed playing and I still enjoyed batting, but I wasn't sure I liked it as much as I had, and maybe not enough to force myself through the ordeal that it had become to sustain a career at that level. I knew there was more to life now. That's probably a very healthy realisation as a person. But as a sportsman, it is fatal.

In the second innings, again trying to score quickly in an attempt to assuage criticism I should not have allowed to enter my mind, I chopped the ball on to my stumps and was out for a duck. I knew I wasn't clear in my decision-making and, as I sat there after the game, celebrating a nine-wicket victory with that young team, I realised my time was up. I was in the way now. It was their time.

My instinct was to retire immediately. Adam Lyth was desperate to play and I felt I was blocking his progress. He was all but certain to be picked in the summer, so it seemed to make sense to give him the chance to gain some experience before that challenge.

I wasn't sure who to talk to among the squad. Cooky had his own issues and, while I knew his door was always open, I didn't want to be a burden to him. At that stage, he still hadn't made the century he required to safeguard his position and he was still hurting having been sacked as ODI captain.

Alastair Cook:

There was no sentiment involved in his selection for the West Indies tour. He earned that place through consistent performances for Warwickshire and then England Lions. I asked Andy Flower who had been the best player on that Lions tour and he was unequivocal with his answer: it was Trotty. He had cleared every hurdle he had been set and he earned that place through merit. Sure, he didn't score the runs he or we would have liked, but I'll always defend that selection.

But it was touch and go whether he played in Barbados. We were very close to giving Adam Lyth a cap, but Trotty had made a fifty in Grenada and we felt that we wanted to give him one more chance. We knew he was battling technical issues, as much as anything, and we knew he didn't look as he used to look.

But we also knew how much of a struggle it had been to get back to that level. We weren't going to discard him without a proper opportunity to show what he could do. It was a bit like giving a debut to a new player: one or two Tests is never really enough time.

In retrospect it was probably a bridge too far. I think his own method ground him down a bit. He always battled against himself. He always did things to excess: the concentration, the drive, the training. He always put himself under pressure and felt failures more keenly than most. Maybe, eventually, it was unsustainable.

He asked so much of himself and, given how much we play and how much pressure we were under, the cracks started to show. The schedule was relentless and, once he had a bad patch, he didn't give himself the chance to recover.

It was a wonderful achievement to get back into the side, though. Really impressive. It showed humility, determination and grit. He showed what a strong man he was and how much pride he had in playing for England. He didn't have anything left to prove to any of us. He left having given it his all. He couldn't have tried harder. We can't ask any more than that, can we?

Peter Moores, too, was under pressure. He had been a controversial appointment. Fired once as England coach, he had just led the team through a terrible World Cup campaign and the calls for his head were growing. I liked Peter. He was clearly a good man and a good coach and it doesn't sit easily with me that his faith in me was counted against him. It felt to me as if he was making progress with that young side, but the awful World Cup campaign was still hanging over him and the last thing he needed was me asking for advice on my future.

So I went back to old friends with Warwickshire and England. I called Jim Troughton and Andrew Strauss by phone and spoke to Mark Saxby, who was with the team. Sax listened – he was never going to tell me what to do. Jim told me to do whatever worked for me; to follow my instincts. Straussy said I should play and give myself a chance to find some form. 'It's one innings since you made a half-century,' he said. 'Don't be so hard on yourself.'

Andrew Strauss:

Leave selecting to the selectors, I told him. I didn't feel, if he pulled out before the final Test, he would reflect on it in years to come as a particularly satisfactory conclusion to his international career.

Having said that, I did also say that, if he was in a situation where he really didn't think he could contribute anything, it was time to put his hand up and admit that candidly.

The key to avoiding such situations in future is managing workload. We do keep an eye out for problems with players and I think the system is better designed to help if problems arise.

But prevention has to be the best cure. So we're very keen to avoid situations where players appear in all formats of the game all the time. It is very difficult to sustain that.

And maybe Trotty has a role here? He hasn't been shy in talking about what he went through and he talks in such a thoughtful, composed manner that he probably can bring some insight to others.

I spoke to Steve Peters, too. Steve maintained that, if I held the course, I would recover and enjoy more success at Test level. But, when I explained to him that I really didn't want to do it any more, he accepted that the decision to retire was appropriate. But he still thought I should play that final Test.

'See the job through,' he said. 'You came back from Australia early. You'll never forgive yourself if you do the same thing again. See the job through.'

I could see the logic in that.

There was another consideration. Just over a year earlier, a few weeks after I returned from Brisbane, I had made a promise to a sick friend that nagged away at the back of my mind. I didn't want to let him down.

Kim Jones had been a loyal supporter from Warwickshire days. Later he owned a cricket magazine, *Spin*, and became a good friend to me, and my wife, when times were tough. He became ill with cancer about the time I came home from Australia and died in January, less than two weeks after he was diagnosed.

It was a brutal end but, in those last days, we had an opportunity to say goodbye. I told him that, when I scored my tenth Test century, I would dedicate it to him. It seemed to give us both hope in those dark times.

It wasn't to be. That tenth century never came and I'm sorry about that. I would have loved to raise my bat to the sky in tribute to him. But as I thought about whether to play in that final match in Barbados, it was a promise of which I was aware. I figured I should take the last chance to honour him in the only way I knew. Even if I scored a hundred, though, it would make no difference. I was going to retire, come what may, after this game.

Anyway, with all those things contributing to my decision, I kept my mouth shut and went into what I knew would be my final Test.

I hardly saw the ball that dismissed me in the first innings. I had walked down the pitch to a short delivery and, instinctively I suppose, raised my gloves to protect my face. The ball lobbed off my hand to the fielder at square leg. Another duck. And another dismissal to a short ball.

The second innings wasn't much longer. I got off the mark – and off a pair – with a nice clip through the leg side off Taylor and actually felt pretty good. My mind was made up; there was a freedom in my play.

But it wasn't to last. Taylor got one to nip back at me, I played across it and they went up for leg before. I knew it was out. Cooky briefly suggested I think about a review, but there was no point wasting it on me at that stage. 'Nah, I'm out of here,' I said.

As I walked off, a group of Barmy Army supporters at the same end as the dressing rooms stood and gave me a warm ovation that was as appreciated as it was surprising for a man walking off having played his last innings of an unsuccessful tour. But they knew it was over and they were, I reasoned, taking the opportunity to say goodbye and thanks. I couldn't raise my bat – I had only scored 9, after all, and England were in a hole – but I gave them a little wave.

I'll forever be grateful for their gesture. They proved, in that moment, that they were true supporters; not fair-weather types who were only there for the good times.

They also proved they had a memory. They remembered the times before I became a stuttering wreck; the times before I wandered towards mid-off before each ball was delivered; the times the only thing people could find to complain about was the manner in which I marked my guard and the time it took us to win Tests.

The good old days.

I didn't want to be remembered like this and I was fearful that in my last four or five Tests I had diluted any reputation I had earned. At a time when things seemed pretty hopeless, I really appreciated that they were understanding and compassionate enough to show they weren't judging me on this version of myself.

Some in the media might not appreciate the Barmy Army but you'll never hear a bad word about them in the dressing room.

As I got into the dressing room, I remember thinking, 'Thank God that's over.' It's a feeling that has never completely gone away. I have no regrets about making the decision to retire.

But I don't regret playing, either. Very few players have the opportunity to say goodbye and those last days within the England set-up gave me closure both on my international career and on a traumatic episode in my life.

An hour or two after the game, with the presentations and formalities taken care of, Peter Moores told the team that I had something I'd like to say.

The room fell silent and I could feel apprehension in the air as I stood up. I wasn't completely sure what I was going to say, but it felt important to mark the occasion. I stood in front of the team, with my cap in my hand, and I started to talk.

I told them I had come to a decision about my future. I told them it had become clear I wasn't able to play at the level I once could and that my time was up. I told them I had been impressed by the talent and spirit I had seen within the squad and that they didn't need me holding up their progress. I told them I believed in them and that I would be supporting them from afar for the rest of their careers. I told them it was their turn now to build a successful England team.

I told them that their England cap was the best thing they would ever wear. I told them how my cap had been soaked in champagne and sweat and tears along the way and that every experience, be it good or bad, had made me appreciate it more.

I wanted them to know how much it had meant to me. How much they had meant to me. And I wanted them to know, however hard they might find it in the future, there were people who they could confide in and people who would understand.

And I wanted to say goodbye and thank you.

We sat together for a few hours that night. It was emotional, but I knew it was right and I knew I was fortunate to leave in that way. Sure, I'd have loved to score that century and I'd have loved to win the game. But I'd been around for long enough by then to know that cricket rarely works like that. My Test career had started with a fairytale; it wouldn't have been fair if it ended in one, too. It almost always has to end badly or it wouldn't end.

Alastair Cook:

There were a few tears in the dressing room when Trotty
made that speech.

We had just had a run where a few guys had won their
100th cap and, while I wouldn't say there was any danger
that anyone would get blasé about playing another Test,
Trotty's words were a timely reminder of how precious
every cap should be. He had been through so much in
between his forty-ninth and fiftieth cap and it reminded
us all what a special achievement it was to represent
England even once.

The emotion of what he said was probably lost on one
or two of the guys who hadn't been in Brisbane, but for
those of us who had been there, who had seen how low
he had been and knew how hard he'd had to dig to come
back, it was an incredibly raw moment. He spoke with
such affection, such reverence for his cap, and said how
proud he was to have played for England and with us as
a bunch of players, that it reminded us all of what we had
been through together, how special it was to represent
this team and why he had been such a great team man
for so long.

I didn't try to change his mind. I could see that it was
the right time for him to go and I thought he had suffered
enough. I wanted him to be released from the pain and
torment that cricket was causing him. I wanted to see him
happy again and international cricket wasn't doing that.

I love Trotty. I mean that. He is a great human being.
Very simple in some ways; very complex in others. He

looks out for quite a few other people and he is quite
simple in his tastes: he loves his family, American sport
and Tottenham. I loved playing with him and I will always
remember those times fondly.

It's sad the way his career petered out a bit, but I hope
people remember what a brilliant player he was. I hope
people remember that, for the first forty-five Tests of
his career, he averaged almost 50 and solved our issues
at number three for about four years. I hope people
remember the century in Melbourne, the century at The
Oval, the century against Pakistan at Lord's. They were
brilliant innings and they deserve to be remembered much
more than the broken man we saw walking off at Brisbane.
That was hardly one per cent of his career and it would be
wrong if it was the image that endured above all others.

Trotty was exactly what England needed. Whether it
is in five years or ten years, he will be one of those guys I
phone up for a chat and I know we'll be friends long into
the future. He's a legend and everyone who played with
him knows that and how much he contributed.

I apologised to James Whitaker. I feared I had made a fool
of him – and Peter Moores – for persuading them to pick
me and then backing out so quickly. They had taken a
chance on me and I'd responded by scoring very few runs
and retiring. It made it look as if their critics were right all
along, and I hated giving them ammunition to use against
these thoroughly decent men. James would hear nothing
of it, but I remain sorry I couldn't repay his faith in the way
we both wanted.

I felt awful for Peter. Losing that Test may well have cost him his job and to have let him down in that way will weigh heavy on me for a long time. He was very well thought-of in that dressing room, both as a man and a coach, and everyone was sorry when they heard the news of his second sacking. It felt, to us at least, as if all the effort, all the work, all the concern for us was starting to pay off, in Test cricket, at least, but he never had the chance to prove it. Sport really is cruel at times.

The mark of the man is how he behaved in those days at the end of the tour. Despite all the rumours about his own job, he never allowed his personal concerns to show in front of us. He was always thoughtful and kind and supportive. He always put us first. When I reflect on my career, it is obvious I owe him a great deal: not least my first international cap and my recall. Again, I wish I could have repaid his faith better.

Over the next few hours, I called my parents. Telling my dad was difficult – I felt I was disappointing him – but my mum was fantastic. She made it as easy as it could have been by saying they respected my decision and that if it was making me unhappy, it had to be the right thing to do. I appreciated that.

Kevin Pietersen:

He phoned me midway through the 2015 season and said he was thinking about retiring. 'Get lost, Trotty!' I said. 'You're far too good to be retiring now. Stop being such a massive idiot. You can still score thousands of runs for

Warwickshire.' I offered to come up to Edgbaston and throw balls at him if it helped.

I honestly believe, if he was managed properly, he could still do a great job for England now. He may have lost a bit of his hunger – and that's fine – but I think he just needed a proper break from the game and some more sympathetic man-management.

We've all been through the anxiety thing. It eats away at you. It stops you sleeping, stops you relaxing, stops you getting the mental break you need to refresh yourself.

It should get easier as you get older. You should worry less and enjoy the game more, safe in the knowledge of what you have achieved. I think it would be easier in the current England side, where you've got a great bunch of guys and a more relaxed coaching set-up. When Trotty was there, you had uptight coaches who just fed the anxiety. A good coach relieves the pressure; ours were the source of it.

It's harder to sustain an international career in England than anywhere because of the English media. They're terrible. They're vicious. They're always calling for someone's head. If you look at South Africa, India and even Australia, some of their best players were given time to finish their careers in the manner they deserved. In England, if you have two bad games, someone is shouting for you to be sacked. It is hard for it not to weigh you down.

My retirement was announced the next day. I declined to do any media and instead slept on a sunbather for a few hours; the sleep of a relieved man. When I woke I had hundreds of messages on my phone. Many were from people with whom I'd shared dressing rooms over the years, congratulating me on my career. There were some great memories and lovely sentiments; I appreciated every one of them. One or two players who had flitted in and out of the dressing room took to Twitter to wish me well, but never sent me a private message. I thought that was a bit odd; some people, it seems, are more interested in being seen to do the right thing by the media and general public than actually fulfilling the image they seek to portray. Those of us who were in the dressing room for a while, though, don't need to do all our talking in public. We know we have a bond; we know we respect one another; we know we're only a phone call away.

I also recall walking back past the pool at the end of the afternoon to go and change before heading out for dinner. Just as we passed a group of England supporters we heard one of them saying, 'If there's one good thing that's come out of this tour it's that Jonathan Trott has retired.'

'How lovely,' Abi said curtly.

To be fair to them, they didn't know we were there and they hadn't meant us to hear. They looked mortified. We carried on walking. I wasn't going to miss that side of the job.

I sometimes joke that I married the first person I met when I arrived in England. It's not quite true – I didn't marry the car hire guy at Heathrow Airport – but it's not far from it. When I landed with Neil Carter ahead of the 2003 season – my first with Warwickshire – we hired a car and drove to Edgbaston. Just as we arrived at the ground, Carts stopped to buy a newspaper and I saw Abi, wearing a Warwickshire tracksuit, for the first time. She was going into the shop at the same time as Carts and they stopped to greet one another. I quickly got out of the car to ensure an introduction.

'Are you the physio?' was the best opening line I could muster, presuming from the tracksuit she must work at the club. She did, too. She was, at that stage, in the marketing department – she was to become the press officer pretty soon – and it turned out she was in charge of deciding who was given a sponsored car. To this day, when she phones me, the contact screen tells me 'Car Lady' is calling. I guess I should change that.

At every stage – whether I was in Warwickshire seconds or world player of the year – she had supported me. She was there, feeding the bowling machine, when I lost my way. She was there, to stick me back together, when I returned from Brisbane. She was there, at The Oval, when I scored a century on debut and there at Bridgetown when I was out for a duck. Whether confronted with triumph or disaster, she reacted with the same calm good humour that pulled me back from despair and kept me grounded from delusions of grandeur. She is the main reason I was able to convert my natural talent into some tangible success. Without the security and certainty she offered, none of it would have happened.

And now here she was at the end. Heavily pregnant with our second child – she had to gain dispensation from the airline to let her travel – she had borne the brunt of the abuse on Twitter, dealt with journalists coming to the door and watched with increasing agony the ordeal as I went out to bat defenceless to combat the missiles coming my way. And, through it all, she had to put up with a husband who was often grumpy, distracted or absent; immersed in my own troubles. It really is worse for the families at times. My brother, Kenny, put it best. The day we won the Ashes in 2009, he remarked that Abi completed me. That seems about right.

Abi:

After that Sussex game, I thought he wouldn't play again. 'I can't take the pain of it any more,' he told me. And I didn't want him to put himself through it if it made him feel so sad. It wasn't worth it.

But one evening a week or so later, he got off the sofa and said, 'I've got to get this sorted.' He called Matt Lawton, the journalist from the *Daily Mail*, and asked him for Stephen Peters' number.

Stephen and Jonathan connected immediately. Jonathan called me on his way home and told me he was going to be OK and, within a few weeks, he was back scoring runs for Warwickshire. He made an incredible recovery.

I know the England return didn't work out exactly as we wanted. But Stephen helped him return to that level. And, more importantly, he gave Jonathan the tools to deal with it when it went wrong. His reaction to it not working out was proportionate. He was disappointed,

of course, but he could see he had done well to get back
to that level and he could cope with it coming to an
end. It wasn't a catastrophe any more. It was just an
international cricket career coming to an end. He could
see he had been lucky to play for so long and that he was
fortunate to call it a day on his own terms.

By the time he finished, watching him had become
agony. I was nervous when he made his debut – of course
I was – but, for a while, I felt confident every time he went
out to bat. When they reached Brisbane, I went to bed
and tried not to think about what was happening. It was
the first time I had ever tried to avoid the coverage. You
can't, of course. I looked at my phone in the middle of the
night and had loads of texts.

By the time he played that last Test in Barbados, I
didn't even go to the ground. We had two rooms in the
hotel with an adjoining door; one for us and one for
Lily. I had the TV on in her room with the sound turned
down and I was in our room, walking in to check how he
was doing every so often. I had excused myself from the
poolside where I had been with other families as I wanted
to be on my own.

I was sad for him when it was over. He worked so hard
to come back and he deserved a bit better. But that's the
game, isn't it?

Most of all, I was overwhelmingly proud of him. To
have had the courage to come back from where he
was, to bat in an unfamiliar position, to be berated and
rubbished and still come back for more. His fiftieth Test
cap is, as far as I'm concerned, his greatest achievement.

Did my return to the England side work out? No. There's no way I can claim it did.

But am I proud of it? Am I proud of challenging myself to climb off the canvas, of facing my fears, of risking failure and of putting myself in the firing line again?

Damn right I am.

You see, in the days before my breakdown – let's call it that – I was generally only required to challenge my sporting ability. But, after the Champions Trophy, after The Oval, after Southampton and Brisbane and Cape Town, I had to challenge myself on an entirely more fundamental level.

I had to expose my vulnerability. I had to challenge myself to fail, to be humiliated, to see my record diluted and hear the accusations of cowardice and selfishness.

I am, odd though it may sound, at least as proud of my final three Test caps as my first forty-eight or forty-nine. It took more courage to go back to Test cricket than it took to get there in the first place. It challenged me in different ways. Ways that extended far beyond backlift or footwork or concentration.

I didn't love everything I discovered about myself. I would have liked to be that guy I had always seen myself as: the one who steps in to calm a crisis; the one who takes charge of the situation; the one who scores the tough runs under pressure. But I wasn't that guy any more, if I ever had been.

But I dealt with the failure. It wasn't a catastrophe. It didn't mean my life was over or that I had brought shame to my family. It just meant I'd played a game and come second. It happens.

My dream had been to finish after the tour of South Africa in 2015–16. I might have wanted to play on for the 2016 summer, but I wanted that to be my last tour. I wanted a chance to emulate one of my heroes, Jacques Kallis, and score a century at Cape Town. I guess I turned out to be a poor man's Kallis. I couldn't bowl as fast as him, I couldn't bat as well as him, I couldn't endure as long as him. He seemed to find it easy to score centuries at Cape Town.

I wanted to score runs in front of all my old friends and make them proud. I wanted to look up at the mountain and remember the boy who had sat with his mum under the oaks on the eastern side of the ground and watched countless afternoons of cricket; the boy who batted for hours on all the pitches and nets in the area; the boy who came through the system at Western Province and went on to be pretty decent for a while. I wanted to put right the situation at the start of my Test career where a family argument had overshadowed what should have been a brilliant, unifying moment for all of us. I wanted – still – for my runs to make everything all right. It wasn't to be.

It hardly ever is. Again, I thought back to Ricky Ponting's struggles during the 2010–11 Ashes. A great player reduced to desperate squabbles with an umpire as he felt his control – his world – slipping away. I wasn't a player in his league, but I could identify with the experience. The game spares no one.

But it has given me a great life. I've travelled the world, made many friends, provided for a healthy, happy family and played in what was, for a year or two, a great team. There are memories and friendships to cherish.

I'm a lucky man. I probably always have been, but now I know it.

EPILOGUE
Lord's, May 2015

I'm a little apprehensive about coming to this game. England are playing New Zealand at Lord's. It's only a few weeks since my retirement from international cricket and I'm not sure if coming straight back to a Test ground might invite back all those feelings of anxiety and even regret. I'm not overly keen on bumping into anyone who might recognise me, either, and I certainly wasn't going to ask for any free tickets.

It was a late decision to come. My agent, James, had arranged to have some early meetings about writing this book. If you're reading this, I guess those meetings must have gone pretty well.

I wasn't sure how I'd feel being back at the great ground. I'd never been here as a spectator before. I wondered if I might feel out of place or awkward or look as if I was trying to hang on to the coat tails of the team I'd left. Nobody wants a batsman hanging around when the umpire's finger has gone up.

I needn't have worried. It's been great. The overwhelming sensation has been of relief. And, freed of the worry of having to go out and perform in front of all these people, I've been able to witness my surroundings with fresh eyes.

What a fantastic ground this is! What a lucky man I've been to play here! And cricket ... what a bloody great game it is! There's no danger of feeling sorry for myself; I feel blessed. Maybe one day my kids – their kids – will come and see my name on the honours board here. That's a nice thought.

Out on the pitch, Ben Stokes and Joe Root are batting beautifully for England. Beautifully and belligerently. How do these guys learn so many strokes? How do they have the confidence to play them in this situation? They came together with England under pressure and are building a substantial partnership. Stokes is quickly developing into the key player for this side while Root, who looked younger than me in my pre-natal scans when he first came into the side, is quickly developing into one of the best players in the world. I'm going to enjoy watching them.

Seeing them play so well has just reaffirmed my decision. These guys are the future. They don't need me getting in the way.

I won't go round to the dressing room. They don't need any reminders about the old days now. I've said my goodbyes; I've closed that door. It's their time now.

I will take the time in the next few weeks, though, to tell Gary Ballance what a fine player he is. I'll tell him how much I rate him and remind him that, if he ever wants a chat, I'm only a call away. He's struggling right now and learning, as I did, how quickly this game can turn from kind to cruel. Maybe he needs a reminder that a few have walked that path before him. Maybe he needs reminding how good he is and how much he has achieved.

I've been asked a few times what I'll do if my kids decide to play cricket professionally. I like to think I'd say 'Brilliant' and give them all the support they wanted. But I also like to think I'd know enough to ensure that wasn't all they did. I'd remind them that they might be a cricketer, but they are also a mum or a sister or a friend or whatever else. Playing cricket should be something they do, not who they are.

So I wouldn't be like that mum who jumped into the ring to join in the boxing bout; I wouldn't be that dad abusing the referee on the sidelines of the football match. I would try and see setbacks and challenges as the sort of tests you need to form a strong, balanced, resilient character. I'd try not to get over-involved and I'd try to learn the lessons from my own career; my own life.

I've not made too many decisions about my future. I guess I'm fortunate that I'm in a position where I can have a year or so to think about it.

I hope that future involves cricket. I've enjoyed the media work I've undertaken so far – I went to the World Cup in Australia and New Zealand for ESPN and the UAE for the Pakistan v England Test series for Ten Sports – and think the experiences I've picked up give me some insight as a coach. I don't suppose I'll be falling back on too many other aspects of my education.

Abi:

Jonathan is a cricketer. I don't mean that as a description of his profession. It extends far beyond that. He is defined by the game. It will always define his mood; it will always be what he is, not just what he does. Cricket has engulfed his life. There's no way back from that at this stage. There hasn't been for years.

Fatherhood hasn't mellowed him, really. It has helped remind him there is more to life than the game, but he will always be a driven person. He will always struggle to deal with what he sees as failure.

Lily is so proud of him. She loves going to watch him and, on his comeback game at Northants, she stood and shouted 'Well done, Daddy' at the top of her voice when he hit his first ball. He only defended it into the off side, I think, but it was such a relief to all of us and she summed it up in that moment.

They recently put a picture of him on the wall at Edgbaston in the area reserved for 'Warwickshire legends'. He hasn't said anything about it, but that means a lot to him. It's his legacy. It shows he has been valued and appreciated in a place that means so much to him.

We had such fun during the time he played for England. We were incredibly lucky to travel the world and have amazing experiences in wonderful places. The friends we made – the memories we made – will last a lifetime. I hope people remember that side of things and don't just focus on the last bit.

In time, I hope he can play a role helping other people

who suffer from similar anxiety issues. The reaction
we had to him doing the Sky interview shows how
little understanding and sympathy there is towards the
condition. He speaks very well about it. I think he could
help.

He maybe isn't there just yet. I think he maybe still
feels a bit of shame or embarrassment talking about
it. In time, though, I think he'll see that is the point: it
needs someone to admit to those feelings. It needs light
shedding upon it.

He'll find his way. Of course he will miss playing and
of course there will be challenges. But he has shown
how strong and resilient he is. He has grown as a person
hugely and is both more self-aware and more aware of
the feelings and challenges faced by others. I wouldn't
quite go as far as saying it's been good for him, but when
you go through something like this, you can learn from it.

Whether coaching or commentating, I will be sympathetic
to those on the pitch. Unlike many former players, I will
never forget how hard it is out there and I will never try to
outdo my fellow commentators with criticism. Some who
cross from playing to the media think the only way they
can earn a living, the only way they can get their voice
heard above the din, is to shock people with their strong
words. If that's what it takes to succeed in the media, then
it won't be for me. But if there is a market for providing a
bit of insight and some constructive analysis, maybe that
is where my future will lie.

Maybe there is a role to be fulfilled in providing a

little more insight into some of the anxiety issues I have experienced, too. The PCA – the Professional Cricketers' Association, the players' union – have made substantial strides in providing support and understanding around mental health issues through their Mind Matters programme. Marcus Trescothick's brave decision to share his experiences of depression has helped change attitudes around that condition, in particular. Perhaps I can help do something similar with anxiety issues? I know it's an issue that extends far beyond the world of sport and I know, from my own experience, that the sense that you are battling it alone is one of the most unsettling aspects of the condition.

But I hope I'm not just remembered for the events surrounding Brisbane in 2013. I played two Tests in Brisbane, you know. And I did OK in the first.

What happened in 2013 is part of my story – an important part – but it's not the whole story. I hope people remember the other parts.

I hope people remember what a good team we were, too. I know the reputation now has been clouded by disagreements and the speed with which it fell apart, but that doesn't reflect how good it was for a while. We played damn fine cricket for a few years. Maybe not for long enough to be defined as a great team, but long enough to be remembered as a very good England side. I hope that's not all overshadowed by subsequent events.

Was it all worth it? Was the brief moment of success worth the agony that followed?

I think so. Most of the time. The game took a lot out of

me, but it gave me back plenty more. But maybe, having read the book, you should decide. There are a few things I would do differently if I had the chance. I'd have taken more breaks, for a start. But to have shared a dressing room with the guys I did and enjoyed the success we did ... I wouldn't change any of that.

And, as I sit here now watching the future of England batting, I feel no lasting regret or shame or any fear for the future. Just pride in the achievements and relief that it's all over. I did my best – I really did – and, for a while, it was enough to help England win a few games.

It's an odd thing looking back on an international sporting career. I'm only in my mid-thirties. With a bit of luck, I have more than half my life in front of me. But I'm pretty sure that, even if I live to be 104, my obituary will be about the things I did between the ages of 27 and 33. I hope there's a bit more to come.

INTERNATIONAL CAREER STATISTICS

Wisden Cricketer of the Year 2011
ICC Cricketer of the Year 2011

BATTING

Tests
52 matches (93 innings)
3835 runs
Average: 44.08
Highest score: 226, v Bangladesh at Lord's, 27–31 May 2010
Centuries: 9
119, England v Australia at The Oval, 20–23 August 2009
226, England v Bangladesh at Lord's, 27–31 May 2010
184, England v Pakistan at Lord's, 26–29 August 2010
135 not out, England v Australia at the Gabba, Brisbane, 25–29 November 2010

168 not out, England v Australia at Melbourne Cricket Ground, 26–29 December 2010

203, England v Sri Lanka at SWALEC Stadium, Cardiff, 26–30 May 2011

112, England v Sri Lanka at Galle, 26–29 March 2012

143, England v India at Nagpur, 13–17 December 2012

121, England v New Zealand at Wellington, 14–18 March 2013

Fifties: 19

One-Day Internationals

68 matches (65 innings)

2819 runs

Average: 51.25

Highest score: 137, v Australia at the SCG, 2 February 2011

Centuries: 4

110, v Bangladesh at Edgbaston, 12 July 2010

102, v Australia at the Adelaide Oval, 26 January 2011

137, v Australia at the SCG, 2 February 2011

109 not out, v New Zealand at the Rose Bowl, Hampshire, 2 June 2013

Fifties: 22

T20 Internationals

7 matches (7 innings)

138 runs

Average: 23.00

Highest score: 51, v South Africa at SuperSport Park, Centurion, 15 November 2009

BOWLING

Tests

52 matches (33 innings)

708 balls

5 wickets

One-Day Internationals

68 matches (10 innings)

183 balls

2 wickets

INDEX